ABOUT **A**LPHABETS

SOME MARGINAL NOTES ON

TYPE DESIGN

by HERMANN **Z**APF

THE M.I.T. PRESS, CAMBRIDGE/MASS.

AND LONDON, ENGLAND

PREFACE for the M.I.T. Press Edition

For a narrative rendered dramatic by its author's own
type creations, a mere preface can do little more than
ring up the curtain on a stage fully set. The time and
space allotted may be enough, however, to tell how a
distant artist with unique credentials swam into the ken
of The Typophiles generally, and of the undersigned
typophile in particular.

Something over 20 years ago I received a letter from
Frankfurt am Main, its envelope addressed in a formal
slender italic of assured regularity and grace. Such an
envelope, as every typophile or calligraphile will know,
is not opened at once; it becomes for the eye a kind of
stage whereon certain familiar characters act out some
strange and subtle variations. I could not guess whose
hand it was. Then on the back flap I saw a printed name
and address of the stranger from Germany whose autobiography I was destined to introduce. Yes, reader, I did at last
open that envelope. It contained a sheet of paper an inch
taller than our business-letter size, bearing a top line
written in crisp cinnamon-brown italics (x-height: 1/8")
giving name and address plus the designation *Buch und
Schriftgraphik,* followed by thirty-four lines in blue ink of
German text in a diminutive italic running hand (x-height:
1/16"), a script of uncommon and delighting clarity. As
Hermann Zapf's ensuing narrative will confirm, he was
at that time art director at the Stempel type-foundry in
Frankfurt; and as its managing director, my friend Walter
Cunz, had just introduced him to my small book, *Calli-
graphy's Flowering, Decay and Restauration* (Chicago:
S.T.A. 1947), HZ was writing to bespeak a copy for him-
self. It was to be paid for by German titles I might wish

to order against the sum involved, since money could not then be sent out of the country, and he had no U.S. acquaintance to seek out a copy. I did what any Typophile would do: I inscribed and mailed him a complimentary copy, and thus began an enduring friendship and collaboration.

There followed many exchanges of letters, books, catalogues, specimens, technical articles and the like. HZ was then completing his monograph on William Morris, and I was able to help in revising the small part of the text that had been printed in English. Every so often he sent proof sheets of further works in progress, until in late 1949 the completed *Feder und Stichel* arrived. This, as I told Walter Cunz, deserved to be reissued with English text, especially as the calligraphic plates (cut in metal by August Rosenberger after HZ's originals) stood ready for further impressions. While decision on this was pending I obtained enough copies of *F & S* to satisfy the demands of The Typophiles and of my students at The Cooper Union and at New York University. When HZ came to New York, late in 1951, the German edition of *F & S* was well-nigh exhausted. His deepest satisfaction came from the knowledge that many young students treasured his book not only as a manual but as an example of fine printing seldom equalled by even the most limited of limited editions. The Cooper Union Museum too celebrated his coming with an inclusive exhibition (his first in America) of his type designs, his printed work and a selection from the fifty manuscript volumes he had written during the decade past. In 1952 *F & S*, 'taught English', made its appearance in New York as *Pen and Graver,* published by Museum Books. The same publisher issued in 1954 a book similar in format, *Manuale Typographi-*

cum, containing a hundred full-page designs executed by HZ with type matter only and using a total of sixteen foreign languages. This too went quickly out of print, as
did the edition simultaneously published in Germany. After fourteen years of work HZ finished his second volume of *Manuale Typographicum,* this time in eighteen languages and with pages vertical instead of horizontal.

If the foregoing lines say much of books, it is because type designs have no independent or detached existence. Types are produced with great effort at great cost, produced for use in printed matter required for learning or study or for industrial or commercial needs. And HZ's supreme concern, whether in writing or in printing, is never the single letter but the fusion of such letters into a working text. He wants these texts to be legible of course, but he seeks something more–that such texts preserve a humane and gracious spirit, as of a superior addressing an equal, or of a man talking with his brother. His scribal works, his type designs and his printed works alike impart this sense of quiet, direct communication. And on an earth daily shrinking in relative size, every smallest item in the communicative process ought to be at once dignified, considerate and gracious. These qualities seem almost native in HZ's every work up to his present age. He would be the first to confess (even at eighty) that he still has much to learn; and the examples on the following pages may suggest a strong alliance between his receptive and his creative powers.

New York, January 1970   Paul Standard

The whole duty
of Typography, as of
Calligraphy,
is to communicate
to the imagination,
without loss
by the way,
the thought or image
intended THOMAS JAMES
COBDEN-SANDERSON
to be communicated
by the Author.

10   *(The closer-set matter is a commentary on the main text)*

Born in Nürnberg on 8 November 1918, I spent my childhood in that factory town. My parents lived in a small
settlement in the city's southern section, and I roved the
bordering woods with my schoolmates and was seldom
to be found at home. I chased butterflies, caught sala-
manders and gathered flowers and stones.

It is always disagreeable to have to write of oneself, so
much easier to compose even a whole novel about others.
I marvel at the idea of the New York Typophiles some
years ago in pursuing this book, especially as in a man of
my age nothing can be known of what the rest of his
coming years have in store for him.
You would naturally like to know whether in my childhood I showed an interest in the 'black art'. And how!
As early as my fourth year the blackened hands of the
chimney-sweep made a great impression on me. To have
such lovely black hands—and without being scolded for
it—that was the truest bliss, and I shortly announced that
I too wished to become a chimney-sweep. To be sure, I
was born in the town of such great writing masters as
Johann Neudörffer, Wolfgang Fugger and Michael Bauren-

feind – Nürnberg was also the birthplace of Rudolf Koch, yet I don't believe in the *genius loci,* in any spirit's presiding over a locality; it no longer exists. Not every singer born in Naples becomes a new Caruso; not every printer in Parma today is a second Bodoni. Nor is the case any stronger if we regard the thousands of Nürnberg-made typewriters as a modern triumph over the once proud writing-master tradition. Neither am I – so far as I know – related to the celebrated Churfürstlich Mainzischen Geheimrat und Kaiserlichen Hofpfalzgrafen' Georg Wilhelm Zapf of Nördlingen, who deserves so well of the history of book printing in the second half of the 18th century. If only I possessed his Bibliotheca Zapferiana! No clues, alas! even among my ancestors!

You may presume in me some precocious early love for letter forms or some outstandingly beautiful handwriting while at school. Well, my school report shows a B in penmanship. A postcard, written on a Rhine vacation in the summer of 1929 and by a miracle surviving the destruction of the last war, would offer scant encouragement to any teacher of lettering to declare (so wretched was the scrawl) that this animated child would one day become a 'lettering artist'. But in some childhood drawings of these first school years I discovered – how consoling – lettered lines in capitals with wildly decorated initials. Here, then, are the first tendencies toward calligraphy, and that is reassuring. My first 'lettering designs' in the year 1930 were no calligraphic art works but rather 'secret documents' – the more crazy and illegible, the better. At that time I had no notion of 'legibility'. In class we exchanged notes written in such secret scripts, decipherable only if one had their code or 'alphabet'. My mother was half distracted over these messages with their mysterious signs which must have had some meaning, but which she simply could not read.

My main interest during school years lay beyond all doubt in the realm of the natural sciences. The physics classes kindled in me a great enthusiasm for things technical. Refined to the last detail, there were built at this time electrical devices, all sorts of warning installations, electric doorbells and the like, surprises that strained every nerve within our dwelling. Nor was there any lack of chemical experiments, though my trials with H_2S (the smelly hydrogen sulphide) somehow failed to produce enthusiasm in either parents or neighbors. This attitude I simply could not understand; perhaps it was only a typical expression of the difference between generations – at least I thought so at the time as I took a rock-bound vow to become an electrical engineer, a vow destined to remain unfulfilled.

My father, a metal worker in a large automobile factory, was crudely discharged in 1933 by the new powers in being, and so became unemployed. Pressed by the economic stringency which had begun earlier for my parents through the world's trade crisis, I had to give up my plan to study at the technical school in the new year. Since I was a good draftsman at school, my teachers advised me to seek an apprenticeship in a graphic process plant as lithographer or color etcher. I copied the names of the Nürnberg graphic plants out of the telephone book, and brought my work and my school records to firm after firm. But unfortunately political factors had in those years become more important to many firms than all the handsome grades and recommendations. So I landed at the last of the phone book's greater graphic-process plants listed under the letter U. My drawings pleased by their careful and exact execution – no political questions – but unfortunately no place as a plate-maker was now available. As I packed up my things I was asked if I would like to try retouching positives. At once I answered yes, without knowing what kind of profession it was. Five minutes later I was hired. I hurried home to consult the dictionary on the nature of a retoucher's activity, and on the following Monday, in March 1934, my apprenticeship began at the Karl Ulrich & Co. printing plant.

The apprenticeship lasted four years. Despite the break-fast running, the daily sweeping-up of the journeymen's places after hours and the many vexations, I did manage to learn a good deal. And what a retoucher could accomplish may be seen from the practice of my plant. We had to transpose on photos the heads of the political potentates of the time; for these had been sawed off the plate but the photos themselves were to be used for making new cuts. People never looked to see whether the background shadows agreed with the lighting on the new head; there was only enthusiasm over the speed of the press in converting an event into print.

My first systematic attempts at writing with the broad-edged pen began in 1935—and so this present volume appears after 35 years of experience in letter forms. The fashioning of letters may to many seem a trifling activity, but whoever has occupied himself with it intensively will properly understand a guest-book entry of 1932 by Rudolf Koch: »The making of letters in every form is for me the purest and the greatest pleasure, and at many stages of my life it was to me what a song is to the singer, a picture to the painter, a shout to the elated, or a sigh to the oppressed—it was and is for me the most happy and perfect expression of my life.«

Since 1936 I have completed a variety of manuscript books and broadsides. With my scant pocket money I bought Rudolf Koch's book, *Das Schreiben als Kunstfertigkeit* (Lettering as a Craft) and Edward Johnston's famous manual, *Writing and Illuminating and Lettering*. With tireless zeal in my spare time I wrote pages upon pages of letters that often left me unsatisfied because the models in the books looked so much better—until one day I discovered I had been holding my edged pen in a false position, whereupon things began to look up. But of course no one who is self-taught can be spared such roundabout journeys. Evenings and weekends I sat at home writing and writing—or rather practising, for the waste basket was always full of written pages. My parents considered me almost out of my senses, father being annoyed by the added cost of electric current occasioned by my work at night. My friends went out for dancing and amusement; I stayed home and bravely drew my letters.

When my apprenticeship ended in 1938 I left my home town of Nürnberg and went to Frankfurt and into the Haus zum Fürsteneck, a studio for lettering and musical notation conducted by Paul Koch, the son of Rudolf Koch. Unfortunately Paul never returned from the 1945 Russian campaign. The Haus zum Fürsteneck was destroyed in a March 1944 air attack. I worked here at typography (the studio had a handpress) and with music notes. I became an independent lettering artist from 1 September 1938, but remained a voluntary fellow-worker at the studio thereafter.

In the autumn Gustav Mori introduced me to the D. Stempel type-foundry. He put at my disposal his unique library

of that trade, and now I began to occupy myself with the

study of historic printing types, with the history of book

printing and the technique of typecasting. In Paul Koch's

studio I had first come into contact with punch-cutting,

but now I began to extend my practical attainments under

the guidance of August Rosenberger, a great master of

this subtle craft, a master among the very few such that

the world today affords.

I had then just turned twenty, and the Stempel type-foundry was just twice my age. Only as I learned with my graver to bring forth the counters from the type metal, often enough pricking my fingers in the process, did I gain an ample respect for type. In early 1939 I designed my first printing type, which later was christened Gilgen-gart. This first product, a fraktur type, had yet to suffer all the diseases of childhood, and the type developed rather slowly. Its thriving was further hampered by the war and the sudden antipathy to fraktur by the govern-ment in 1941. The first trial cutting was ready in 1941, but the working sizes were found too unquiet, and the story began all over again. Some caps for the small sizes were narrowed and the lower case simplified by omis-sion of the decorative strokes.

(17) Calligraphic alphabet with Greek capital letters
in an ornamental arrangement.

A new printing type has a long, often thorny way to completion. Before a type has come far enough to please outsiders, it adds gray hairs to its co-producers. Important in the matter is the type's design; a long time is needed to perfect all its details. The imaginary notion of letters from A to Z does not itself suffice, and by the time these more or less vague proposals and fancies attain a definite form, all may look quite different on printed paper. A design needs not just any forms, but good forms that harmonize with the remaining shapes, all distinguishable as signs and of noble character. In addition come technical considerations that must be thought through. Many a letter seems to strain against a form it dislikes. Alas! it is tamed. Ever and anew it undergoes revision in black and white until it willingly accommodates itself to the higher conformity of the type fount. What designer in the development of his drawing does not know those spooky, stubborn antipathetic shapes that, maverick-like, will not join the type family? They still dream of the freedom of their revered ancestors in the older scripts whose sweeps knew no trammels. There is, for example, the familiar f, or especially *f* in an italic type, both asking patience and giving trouble; and rather often g and r and other letters become no less trying.

At last, after long toil, the design shows all the characters ranged bravely and amicably together, and full of pride in his handiwork the designer delivers his work to the type-foundry. If he is lucky—or rather very lucky—his clients are at once satisfied. But often they have many ifs and buts, and once again begins the game of black and white on the paper battleground. Here and there the forms are somewhat pinched off, many a spirited flourish must with heavy heart vanish. The art of omission is surely the hardest and yet so essential, but no art expert has yet written a book about it. At last the type design is usable, and work can start on a trial cutting. There are many ways to convert the graphic artist's portrait of the letters into the letters of lead for the printer. In earlier centuries every letter was cut by hand in steel – a hard task this, by craft and subtlety to bring a tiny form to the surface of a bit of steel – for what the graver had cut away to excess was gone forever. But it is said that people in those days had more quiet and the times were not so exciting as the twentieth century; perhaps we delude ourselves with this for the sake of the solace it brings. The old masters of the art of punch-cutting had in any case the necessary patience. Their previously hardened steel punches were struck into little copper stumps which were then ground to precision or, as the craftsman would say, were justified. Thus are matrices prepared for the casting of the letters of lead.

Where today a type is still cut by hand – usually in only a single size, the so-called standard size – this is seldom cut in steel, but in an alloy of lead. The advantage is that being much softer and more easily worked, lead makes corrections easier. Anything cut away can be soldered on. In our mechanized age the machine soon conquered more and more of the type production field. Machines working with hardly imaginable precision took over the work of the hand punch-cutter. The designer's drawing is brought photographically to the needed working size, and from it a metal pattern is made. According to the machine's construction, either a raised metal pattern (for the punch-cutting machine) or a flat pattern (for the matrix-engraving machine) is used. In the case of the flat pattern the letter's contours are deeply engraved. The machine works on the pantographic principle, so that varying adjustments will produce varying type sizes from a single pattern. As the name implies, the punch-cutting machine produces a punch (patrix), either of steel or type metal. The steel punch is then stamped into a softer metal (pressed into the brass matrix), or the type-metal original by galvanic process creates a matrix (electrotype master). The matrix-engraving machine, on the other hand, engraves the matrix by cutting directly into the brass (engraved matrix). After justification, casting can begin.

All await impatiently the proof of the first letters. They are seemingly transformed on the paper, now at last appearing in their native character to the designer. They seem either pure, graceful, true of image, quite as he conceived them; or knavishly grinning, awry, as if out of insolence ready to fall on their faces, or too gaily hop-dancing on the line, wilful, unregarding of their neighbors; still others are unduly fat or plump or again too spidery, too meager and wretched in expression. Others on the contrary have bumps on their curves, lame arches, lack tension or expression on the line. The initial joy is thus cancelled by critical reflection and comparison with the original drawing. Only thereafter is it worth trying to disarm the objections and the defensive orations of one's technical co-workers. The first immaculate impression is now scrawled with corrections and ameliorations, the fearsome red pencil goes into action and many a letter is quite rejected and must be made anew. It is now a dogged tussle over form, the designer on the one side armed only with pencil and pen, and on the other his numerically superior opponents, fully mechanized and equipped with machines of utmost refinement. Woe, if the machine wins out and the characters are shaped after its judgment! Who will then need to wonder if the emergent letter is cold and soulless?

Much time passes before every letter is reshaped and all the participants' faces look satisfied. In the end, the new child must have a name, and this too occasions much brain-wracking, since it must be a handsome name well suited to the character of the new creation, a name naturally not yet used by any other type-child. If the parents are agreed and summon some celebrated godfather from history or a sonorous name drawn from the purest fantasy, the happy event will be expectantly advertised to an unsuspecting world of book printers. According to the parent's means, the official type-specimen form of the birth-announcement assumes a modest or a grand appearance. Soon enough one encounters the type in printing offices, where it may be puffed up with pride as it supplants its dust-covered rivals.

For the printer there is joy or vexation ahead, according as the face proves itself durable, useful and economical, or on the other hand the type is overdelicate, its beauty fading too soon. So much often depends upon sympathy, which can change as quickly as a freak of fashion, since the chief may already be flirting with another type. Such a new face may frequently be accorded an equal rank with the other; what a monstrous challenge! And if fate puts both faces into the same printed job they bite each other or, as the saying goes, the one 'kills' the other. And while things do not always sink to such sadness in a printing office, yet what becomes of decency and respect? One hears of a compositor's having one afternoon mislaid the 'fat Eve', while a colleague had laid aside the 'light Venus' (both girls here being only types). Yes, that's how

compositors treat types and 'our children' as well; and
what strange things they create. A century ago Wilhelm

Junk summed it all up in the words: »What a crop of
rubbish is daily printed by the possible regrouping of
only 25 letters.«

The fateful year 1939 brought no very quiet time for me

either. From April to September I had to render the

'Reichsarbeitsdienst' (labor service) on the border forti-

fications of the Rhine Palatinate. Then came the war with

all its terror.

In early 1939 the Bärenreiter-Verlag commissioned of me

a music type for two-color printing, and the casting was

duly made in the Stempel type-foundry. Only a few trial

proofs of this Alkor-Notenschrift were printed before it

was lost in the war. To this same year belong also the de-

signs for the lettering book *Feder und Stichel*. The book

comprises twenty-five alphabets and calligraphic pages,

and I finished work on it in 1941. During the war years

August Rosenberger cut the plates with all care by hand

in lead, and even today I marvel at his patience and his

assiduity in doing so laborious a task in spare time at

home between air-raid alarms and trips to the shelter.

I was drawn into military service at Weimar, and in the

following year I came as a map designer to a cartographic

unit in France, first in Dijon and later in Bordeaux, where

in 1943 I began my drawings for *Das Blumen-ABC* (Flower

Alphabet). These too were cut in metal by August Rosen-

berger during the war, though it was only in 1948 that

all the cuts were completed.

If my 'Reichsarbeitsdienst' in the summer of 1939 was for
me no joyous time, I had it no better in the army. I still
recall how as a raw recruit on the drill-ground I once
grasped the tail of a field howitzer's gun-carriage with a
delicacy reserved for my Chinese brush or my pen: my
battery commander got almost a fit of raving madness
and drove me from the barracks-yard. I landed in the
office and got—my pen!
From my soldiering days I still have my three sketch-
books, made in my scant free time. They show no heroic
battle scenes, but rather lettering exercises, watercolors
of flowers I found during my brief freedom in the barracks-
yard, or sketches of the towns through which I passed

(24/25) Drawing for the Narrow Linotype Aldus. The smoke proofs
of the trial letters 9 pt. pasted up for comparison.

mue

↑ Normal - Linie

Die Versalien sind
absichtlich
steiler

BKN

m

H

→g←

pgq

ⓐ

aot

s

rund?

Größe der Akzente

H'kf

f

rund?

amburg *Hamburg*

Mabefgkmoprstubo

MabefgkmoprstuBar

Januar 1960   ok

2. Oktober
1959

until the war ended. They constitute a somewhat unsoldierly 'Service Record' in the eyes of my superiors, especially when one realizes that a soldier catches butterflies or stag-beetles in the acacia forests of southern France because he needs them as models for his drawings in a *Blumen-ABC*. The nature of some of my reflections for 1942 may be gathered from a Goethe passage entered in brown ink in one of my sketch-books: »It is as if the world existed for the brutal and the overbearing, while the quiet and the reasonable must beg a tiny place by the grace of God.«

In the spring of 1945 following an illness, I was sent to a Heidelberg hospital; just before the war's end I was sent to Tübingen, and then as a prisoner of war to an infirmary in the Black Forest. By early June I was released from my confinement as a French prisoner of war and returned to Nürnberg to my parents. At first I had scant inner calm for the making of lettering designs. I drew for myself, and only in the autumn resumed my activity as independent commercial artist, and finished the last designs for the *Blumen-ABC*.

In 1947 I moved again to Frankfurt to assume the artistic

direction of the house printing-office of the D. Stempel type-foundry. I had earlier (1946-47) taught lettering for the first time in Nürnberg; and in 1948, along with my job at the Stempel foundry, I accepted an instructorship in lettering at the Werkkunstschule in Offenbach am Main, formerly known as the Kunstgewerbeschule, in which Rudolf Koch had once taught. But as my work at the type-foundry kept increasing, I had to give up my Offenbach instructorship in 1950.

I once came upon this apothegm of Gottfried Wilhelm Leibniz: »The man who has taught the ABC to his pupils has accomplished a greater deed than a general who has won a battle.« This was a comment upon teaching in general; yet even 200 years after the great philosopher's death such views have yet to find universal acceptance. In any case, generals still seem to me more honored and better paid than are teachers and professors.

For inspiration's sake I went to Italy in the autumn of 1950. With sketchbook and camera I sought old Roman inscriptions in Florence, Pisa and Rome, and the encounter with these letters and with the splendid books in the Laurenziana and in the Vatican Library greatly influenced my later work. Every lover of beautiful letter forms will understand how transported I was by the inscription on the Trajan Column, erected in the Foro Traiano, Rome, in 114 A. D.; but the panel is set so high as to make impossible an undistorted photo. Apparently I had only too visibly shown my interest in the Trajan Column, for a policeman suspected, from my climbing about with my tape-measure, that I was about to take the whole inscription down to ground-level.

In 1946 I began work on a new roman type for the Stempel foundry. The trial cuttings made for this face, named Novalis, were finished in 1948 in the 10 point size, along with two companion weights in italic and in bold. I had started in 1948 another roman, based rather on Renaissance models; this face, lacking the edged-pen emphasis of the Novalis, was more suited to a broad field of utility printing, because it reflected modern feeling and its open counters seemed more adapted to offset and letterpress printing. The designs were ready in 1948. Work on the Novalis type was thereupon abandoned and all was concentrated on the new roman, which was to have been named Medici, but this was changed to Palatino. The studies and sketches of my Italian visit were converted

into the Palatino type family, their very names suggesting

their Italian models.

Well, may the reader ask, why always new types when there are already so many and the choice becomes more difficult and complex for the poor printers? A counter-question might be, why always faster motor cars (a mail-coach journey 150 years ago was too speedy for Goethe), and why even faster composing machines and printing presses? All becomes faster—only mankind's reason seems at times not to keep pace with modern development. As the reader generally cannot distinguish between the 'old familiar faces' and the new, his question seems justified, since we ought to be able to get along with the types already available. Finally, type designers cannot always think up something new. Some decades ago, the noted American type designer Frederic W. Goudy—surely the greatest type designer of recent times—came to the conclusion that »the old fellows stole all of our best ideas«. What shall we say today, since Goudy himself made over 100 different printing types up to his death in 1947? When Claude Garamond and Giambattista Bodoni created their famous printing faces (for us still 'archetypes') all printing was done entirely with the hand press upon dampened hand-made paper. Their types had to meet only these requirements. Today, on the contrary, a useful printing type must be suited not only to the content and surface finish of the various printing papers (and what do not the paper mills mix into their paper-brews today!), but suited also to the refined demands of modern high-speed presses. And it must further do justice to the newer processes—offset and gravure, and stereotypes and electrotypes for large runs on rotary presses. The type itself is no longer hand-cast as in earlier centuries, but in fast-running type-foundry casting machines; or in elaborately-devised composing-machines, casting either a complete line or single letters. In the electronic photographic way of composition, the letter is destined to an unimaginable speed in reproduction. These problems surely never afflicted Garamond and Bodoni. A modern type will hence avoid narrow counters (producing narrow inner areas in the letters), such as appear in Garamond's e, or the delicate hairlines of Bodoni's or Didot's types. Whoever has heard a printer's explosive language when the tender serifs break in printing (since hardly anyone today takes time or care or patience to replace broken letters), will dream of a type that will not needlessly tax the printer's spiritual equilibrium. All these simple examples will have suggested two fundamental requirements in the design of a new type especially for the smaller sizes: open and clear letter forms and a well-defined weight of stroke for the modern technical demands additionally made by the newer technical processes.

By 1950 the Palatino face was destined for extension into

a type family. It comprises to date over a dozen different

founts as shown in the 1953 and 1960 Palatino specimen

books of the Stempel type-foundry. The first important

work composed in Linotype Palatino was the *Gutenberg-*

Festschrift to mark the 50th year of the Gutenberg-Gesell-schaft in Mainz in 1950, the hand-set Palatino being first used in the same year in Stempel's special edition of *Feder und Stichel*. A second edition of *Feder und Stichel* appear-ed in the Trajanus-Presse, the private press of D. Stem-pel AG (Insel-Verlag) in 1952, and in the same year was published its first edition in English (New York: Museum Books), edited, introduced and translated by Paul Stan-dard. Along with the Linotype Palatino italic (its width of body matching that of its roman), there was also issued in 1949-50 a narrower Palatino italic for hand-setting, this being completed in 1952, including supplemental swash characters.

My inscriptional studies, with which I returned from Italy in the autumn of 1950, became a great stimulus, espe-cially to the titling types Michelangelo and Sistina. Before the end of 1950 the slender Michelangelo was already cut; the more powerful Sistina followed in 1951, and the

Sistina poster type (up to 240 point) in 1953. Since the Palatino family was intended mainly for display, it became essential for optical reasons to use a most careful gradation of scale in the weights of the several sizes. The ratio of capital height to thickness of main stroke in the Michelangelo becomes 1:12, in the Aldus 1:11, in Palatino 1:9, in Sistina 1:7 and in Palatino Bold 1:5. The somewhat calligraphically-stressed letters E F S q p s v w and y in the Palatino roman were given more traditional forms for the British and American markets—forms derived essentially from conversations with Franz C. Hess, Huxley House, in New York and with the American type designer, W. A. Dwiggins, Hingham, Mass. Also my friend Paul Standard of New York, who has always shown exceptional interest in my types and my scribal work, has often influenced my practice by his critical observations, and I have much

(33) Drawing 36 pt. Palatino redrawn for Linotype Aldus to get smaller proportions.

¶ÄBCDEFG

HIJKLMNQPRST

UVWXYZÆŒ

ra   1²1234567890

åbcdèfghijklmnö

pqrstúvwxyz &ß

[(† . · - = , ! ? „ » * §

EFUŴ

to thank him for. A later extension of the Palatino family

—the designs were made in 1952—resulted from a suggestion of Gotthard de Beauclair. This special book-face, renamed Linotype Aldus Buchschrift, was produced in 6 to 12 point sizes with italics and small caps for the 1954 Drupa exhibition. The Aldus was cut in steel in all sizes in a friendly collaboration with Arthur Ritzel, in charge of the punch-cutting department at Stempel, wherein no supplemental corrections whatever were needed. Frankly a text type, a bit slimmer and more delicate than Palatino, Aldus found its first use in Hugo von Hofmannsthal's *Reden und Aufsätze,* constituting volume No. 339 in the popular Insel-Bücherei series. During 1959-60 a new fount of Aldus was designed, some ten per cent narrower on the body but still eminently readable. With all these faces, Palatino is now the most varied type family among roman types based on renaissance models.

Many printed items have since been set in Palatino and in Aldus types, beginning with the 1957 annual report of the Standard Oil Company (New Jersey) in an edition of over 600,000 copies and proceeding to the countless German pocket volumes published by Rowohlt, by S. Fischer and other publishers. But my own wedding announcement of 1951 I printed not in Palatino, but chose instead a 'competitor type', the Diotima. (Designed by Gudrun von Hesse.)

My Melior type appeared in 1952. As far back as 1947, I had received the task of designing for the Linotype a new newspaper roman exceptional for easy legibility. Preparatory work and designs for the Melior type series date from 1948, and trial cuttings began in 1949. During my first stay in New York in 1951 I studied some findings of the Mergenthaler Linotype Company in Brooklyn which are concentrated upon the field of newspaper type practice, so as to apply its benefits to Melior. Up to 12 point, Melior is now available on the Linotype, with added display founts in italic or in bold founts. For hand composition the face has now been carried to the 60 point size with further bold condensed founts for newspaper head-

lines, these types being designed in 1949 and released in

1952. The first German daily to appear in Melior type was

the *Hannoversche Presse* with its issue of 1 November

1952.

While revisiting the United States in 1954 and 1957, I often talked with friends about printing types and modern industrial design. It seemed odd to find ultra-modern folk there for whom a plane that needed nineteen hours to fly from Frankfurt to New York was already a hobbling vehicle, but who in their own printed works preferred the most old-fashioned types of the 19th century. How one wished to ask these fanatics of 'progress' whether they still drive cars built in 1900, or furnish home or office in turn-of-the-century style. (In my little Optima pro-spectus of 1959 I have pointedly shown an old American auto, in order to tease such folk and perhaps induce re-flection.)

The type of today and of tomorrow will hardly be a faith-ful recutting of a 16th century roman of the Renaissance, nor the original cutting of a classical face of Bodoni's time—but neither will it be a sans-serif of the 19th cent-ury. It will surely be said that most book printers and their customers demand the historical forms. But on the other hand most of the public, too, demands cheap imita-tions of Chippendale furniture, Renaissance writing tables and romantic reproductions. Nor is it always only the little people for whom modern forms lack appeal, since taste only too often fails to keep pace with the growth of the bank account. Progress always demands courage; and as the powers of conservatism were and are always in the majority, they will not stop the entire development, they can only retard it. But where do we stand today? There is much talk of modern design, but if we study the catalogues and promotional printing we often find late 19th century printing types being used to promote these 'modern forms'. Just to which point in the 19th century do our lives and endeavors seek to return? Can the second half of the 19th century, the time of stylistic confusion and historicism, offer any basis for a future development? One has only to think of railway stations with Doric columns of iron, and of the neo-gothic churches, or simply of the ample beards of our great-grandfathers.

Begun as a major type project in 1952, it was only in 1958 that the Stempel foundry and the German Linotype could jointly show, at the Drupa exhibition in Düsseldorf, the sans-serif roman named Optima. It was designed, after years of study and trial, to accompany the Palatino-Melior group. Visiting Italy in 1950, I brought along some sketches of alphabets I had drawn after inscriptions on the Arch of Constantine (315 A.D.) and on gravestones in the Santa Croce in Florence: unserifed letters that delighted me by their simple, vigorous forms. Several of these letters of

inlaid marble, dating from the Quattrocento and largely

unregarded by visitors in the Santa Croce, set me to

thinking that their austere forms might through deeper

study emerge as a useful printing type. A design for Op-

tima was ready by 1952, but it took until 1954 to complete

the models in all essentials. A conversation in October

of that year with Monroe Wheeler of The Museum of

Modern Art in New York proved so convincing that I

changed my original notion of Optima as a display type

more into one of a text type; and now that I see it com-

plete, I believe this type can be profitably used with

photos and industrial presentations in books and catalo-

gues. The result was an eminently practical roman with a

destined area of utility in books of art or photography,

in technical or scientific publications, and in children's

books and periodicals. As against other types with oblique stress growing out of edged-pen techniques, Optima

has the advantage that it can be mixed with a great variety

of other types.

The idea of Optima is based upon a serifless roman. Its difference from a so-called grotesk or sans-serif appears most clearly if we examine the structure of the latter forms. Their alleged principle of uniform weight of stroke is grotesquely ignored save in only a part of the alphabet. Many characters must for optical or technical reasons show thinnings where an arch joins a stem, since otherwise these junctions become too dark. Rather is Optima built on the principle of alternating weights of stroke (as in Walbaum, for example), and the type shows throughout its curves a constant axial direction, a structure logical and consistent.

This principle of a serifless roman is no modern version of a Grotesk. Numerous historical examples from past centuries, indeed even early Greek inscriptions, show serifless letters made with alternating stroke-weights, but this principle has hitherto scarcely been applied to text types. Printed and stamped trials as well as photographic reproductions were made of Optima before even the first size was cut. With Edward Rondthaler of Photolettering Inc. New York, I made trials for the italic by means of his precise and flexible photo-lenses. Further investigation of Grotesk types showed that their small sizes lost their sharpness rather quickly and became rounded through their wearing-off in printing. I accordingly strengthened Optima's main strokes and the outer contours of some letter's terminals to assure greater resistance to wear or

(40/41) Capitals of the italic version for the Narrow Aldus
with alternatives for E, F, U and Y.

A ?

ACD

Q ?

LNQ

UWX

 evt. normale U als II. Form?

(b)

EFGJ

J
als
II. Form
?

F als
II. Form?

PRST

U?

YZ

Januar 1960

* für E und F

ok
27.1.60

deformity occasioned by long runs and in the newer processes of printing. Such reinforcement further softened

optically the stiffness of a serifless form, which had given
my first designs a more tedious look. The type is therefore, despite its objective impersonal character easily and
pleasantly legible. This subtle strengthening at top and
bottom already appears in old Roman inscriptions, which
we–let us be honest–emulate even today.

In sizes above 14 point, Optima was not to have the un-
lovely short descenders that deface other roman types
which hark back to the German 'normal type-line' estab-
lished in 1905. To preserve due proportions, by the
Golden Section, between the x-heights of the small letters (minor) and the ascenders and descenders (major)
I have, in each of the sizes above 14 point, raised the
baseline by full points. What this means–that is, the chang-
ing of a law privileged in Germany through fifty years'
acceptance by conservative type-founders and printers–
can hardly be exaggerated. The ratio of capitals to the
x-heights of the small letters accords, besides, with the
'Golden Typographic Proportions' developed by the research of my friend Raúl M. Rosarivo of Buenos Aires. The
Linotype sizes of Optima roman with its italic and its bold
all stand on the normal type-line level; and its founts of
bold condensed, owing to their proportions, are also on
the German normal-line. Optima's neutral design permits good combinations with many available display types
–and what all is not being mixed in composing rooms
today, the most impossible mixtures everywhere!

Sales considerations being generally decisive when a type
is named, the child occasionally acquires a rather sonorous but fundamentally unsuitable name. Not every Sieg-
fried is a hero, and a Cornelia may seem unlikely ever to

become a gentle maid. A fat Venus is to others quite different-looking than to a compositor. So it seemed imperative, in view of the calligraphic character of Palatino and especially of its italic, to name this type after the 16th century Italian writing master Giovambattista Palatino, a contemporary of the Frenchman Claude Garamond, since its letters more suggested roman types of the Italian Renaissance than French models. The original Leichte Palatino Buchschrift was later renamed Linotype Aldus Buchschrift for the famous Venetian book printer. But it nevertheless represents no historical copy or even recutting of any book face of Aldus Manutius, despite its name. The name Melior seemed proper and useful for a newspaper type, though at first it was called Columbia, and Tempora. For a serifless roman, on the other hand, I should have liked a less pretentious name than Optima, a name that should more justly express the striving for simplicity. Upon the original drawing of Optima appears the designation 'Neu Antiqua', a name I had myself desired.

The Stempel type-foundry in 1952 brought out Virtuosa,

a script type. The available English (round hand) script

faces with their delicate joins and hairlines are basically

untypographic, since they signify a 19th century attempt

at imitating lithographic scripts. But the elegant written

strokes of the lithographer can be adapted to book print-

ing only by a complicated system of casting. As far back

as 1947 and 1948 I had begun sketches for a script face

more suited to the rules of typography. I had long wanted

to work out a script type without direct joins, stronger in

the hairlines than the so-called English script types, and

avoiding all great kerns. It took until the end of 1952

before the first sizes of Virtuosa were ready. A simplified

form of the caps named Virtuosa II was added a year

later, with Kräftige Virtuosa (Virtuosa Bold) following in

1954 at the Drupa exhibition.

The great success of this script type, lacking joins and
dispensing with delicate hairlines, brought many similar
types to the market since 1952, so that too many printers
would not use only the Virtuosa founts of the Stempel
foundry in Frankfurt am Main. At any rate this competi-
tive zeal confirmed the truth of my technical reflections
upon the three Virtuosa types.

In 1953 I began to adapt the classical Greek meander

(key pattern) for use in borders. Working drawings were

finished in 1954 and it was another year before the first

series of these meanders, designated Attika Borders, were

available for composition. Despite all objective aims, typographic ornament remains an important part of com- positional form. In 1948 I designed a series which was cut from 1949 to 1951 and came out as Primavera Ornaments. A great variety of lines, more freely and graphically formed for the manifold needs of advertising, were worked out in 1954 and put in production in 1955 under the somewhat pretentious name of Artist's Lines. Another series may be mentioned, of new astronomical signs which appeared in 1950, and some English ornamental rules of brass to serve as border units.

Back in 1940 I had tried to design, in 36 point, a meander ornament of severe, purely linear structure, since all meanders for typesetting were purely geometric in form. After many trials I gave up the task because I could not then find a reasonably useful and simple way of fitting the corner-pieces. This very problem of corner-pieces for meander borders had given the old master Bodoni much trouble, and I consoled myself that things had gone no better for him. At last only a freely-drawn line, which I used in my designs of 1953, made it possible to obtain satisfactory solutions for those queer corner-pieces. Even

so, there were many anxieties, trial castings and recon-
siderations before the seemingly self-evident meanders
of the Attika Borders were ready for use.

In 1954, at the Drupa show in Düsseldorf, the type Kompakt made its first appearance—a type of accentuated
contrast which I had designed in 1952. The Festlichen
Ziffern, or Festival Figures (designed 1948, released 1950),
and Saphir, the roman titling decorated in like style (designed 1950, released 1952) may be regarded as a modern
version of Fournier's decorated types. The design of Saphir
was actually intended for smaller sizes that were not
completed; and its forms in the larger sizes available seem
a little crude and inelegant.

The Stempel foundry in 1953 needed for its Greek market
supplemental Greek designs for these types: Light Neuzeit-Grotesk, Semi-Bold Condensed Neuzeit-Grotesk,
Virtuosa (as a Greek script type), and a new Greek face
to complete the available roman. This new Greek 'roman',

as we must call it, was to be based not on the usual neo-

classic forms, but rather on the various classic romans in

the Renaissance style. (Garamond, Palatino, Aldus and

the like.) What served as its basic model was the hand-

written *Heraklit,* reproduced and published as Insel-

Bücherei volume No. 49. This Greek face took from that

title its name Heraklit, the first sizes being finished in

1954. Insel's edition for the year 1957 (11th - 17th thous-

and) was not reproduced again from my manuscript pages

of Greek, but was newly composed in the new Heraklit

type. Heraklit's first actual use was in 1955 in my own

design of a German-Greek Bible for the international

Liber Librorum project. In 1959 Heraklit was further used

(together with Optima) to set the catalogue of the Ger-

man Book Exhibition in Athens. The supplementary Greek

Neuzeit-Grotesk appeared at the end of 1953 under the

names Attika and Artemis. And the Greek script type on

the lines of Virtuosa was ready in 1954 and was baptized

48 Frederika. As I had already in 1952 designed the supplementary Greek characters to my Michelangelo type, they appeared in 1953 as Phidias.

The Linotype showed, at the 1954 Drupa, a neo-classic roman which the company commissioned me to design. Because of the hundredth birthday of Ottmar Mergenthaler, the inventor of the Linotype, this face was named Linotype Mergenthaler Antiqua.

How I plagued myself in 1953 to do justice to an assigned task—namely, to create a neutral, impersonal type suited for scientific work and compressed catalogue setting, and allowing for accents in foreign languages! I designed for this purpose a roman, a companion italic, and a bold for display. The pity is that this whole effort is not fully seen, and everyone thinks only, what an impersonal type this is. For who can know all the host of technical considerations that the newer Linotype faces demand? Optima, for instance, was so devised that its Linotype 8, 9, 10 and 12 point sizes in the Teletypesetter system could be set with a multiface perforator and its counting magazine. This type can also, without redesign for photo-composition, be used on the Linofilm. Since in the Teletypesetter and Linofilm systems the single let-

(49) Optima Roman. Foundry proof-sheet of 36 pt. (November 8, 1958) with corrections for the casting.

36 p Optima Nr. 5699

ABCDEFGHIJKLMNOPQRS

TUVWXYZ

ÆŒÇÄÖÜÅØ & MN

abcdefghijklmnopqr r

stuvwxyz chckfffiflftß

|a|b|c|d|e|f|g|h|i|j|k|l|m|n|o|p|q|r|

|s|t|u|v|w|x|y|z| æœçäöü

åøáâàéêèëíîìïijóôòúûù

.,:;!?„"-'—»«//*†[(§)]

$1234567890£

The Museum of Modern Art

D. Stempel AG 8.11.1958

Zurichtung vom C nachprüfen

Rundung verbogen ebenso beim Œ und Œ

diese Partie ist zu leicht

jetzt ok

Bogen nicht gut

r evt. etwas breiter

obere Partie zu leicht

?

Bogen schlecht

rund

Ligatur ij in der Weite nachprüfen

Zurichtung Ziffer 4?

12. 11. 1958

Zurichtung vom M nachprüfen

ters must be provided for by means of calculable units, the establishment of the letter-widths was a fresh limit-
50 ation and aggravation in the working-out of Optima. In the cutting of their types, Claude Garamond and Bodoni never had to agonize over such prodigies of calculation.

In 1954 the need arose to cut a new Arabic type for ex-

port. This was no easy task, since in this type the custom-

ary kerned characters were to be avoided, to make the

new Arabic more useful for newspaper composition than

the founts hitherto used. Along with one's own ideas

which as type designer one may often pursue for years in

historical examples that are studied, rejected, reshaped

and ever anew resumed, many interesting tasks arise from

the special demands of a world-wide type-foundry such

as D. Stempel AG. Often these require intensive study,

particularly when the matter concerns foreign types.

I had occupied myself since 1945 in the study of Arabic

letter forms (in the so-called Naskhi style), while within

my calligraphic exercises I completed as my fiftieth manuscript the Book of Suleika from Goethe's *West-Östlicher Divan*. Prof. Dr. Joseph Hell of the Oriental Seminar at the University of Erlangen gave me the needed instruction and references. To be able to design a new type, I had to go deeper into the manner of writing the Arabic letter forms, and I busied myself for weeks on end with oriental calligraphy and with the extant Arabic printing types cut since the 16th century. Not every reader may know that Goethe too had occupied himself with Arabic signs in connection with the *Divan,* as appears in a letter to Christian Heinrich Schlosser, dated 23 January 1815: »As to the *Divan,* little is lacking that I should learn Arabic, too; at least I shall so far practice the written characters as to be able to render the amulets, talismans, abraxas and seals in the original script. In no other language, perhaps, are spirit, word and script so organically fused together.«

Naturally I awaited in great excitement the judgment of Stempel's agency in Teheran, as at the end of 1954 my designs were dispatched for approval. My work found a very positive agreement, and my drawings needed virtually no changes. Work could now begin on the cutting. The first size of Alahram Arabic was ready at the beginning of 1956, and a shadowed fount followed a year later. Arabic alphabets are still used today in lands reaching from North Africa into India.

My first acquaintance with the Arab world came more by compulsion and accident than I wished or willed. As I laid in a Black Forest hospital with a Tunisian in May of 1945, out of boredom and as a useful pastime I learned from him not only Koran verses in Arabic but Arabic written characters as well. In early June of 1945 I was sent directly home from the hospital, but unfortunately fell into the hands of a French scouting party consisting of a Tunisian and a Moroccan, who took my discharge papers as a French prisoner of war, and without reading them set about shooting me. An Arabic aphorism, learned in my hospital days, saved my life at the last moment: »One good man should not kill another good man«. An exciting adventure for me; one I would rather not relate in greater detail.

With the end of 1956 I withdrew from the art director-
ship of the D. Stempel type-foundry, in order to devote
myself entirely to my work as book and graphic artist,
since the demands of a business organization in person-
nel matters and in the many administrative tasks tend to
grow in extent from year to year.

For the Linotype in Frankfurt I have since continued to
supervise the production of its types. Worthy of mention
is the putting of Janson roman on the German Linotype
in 1951. The work on this historic type became the more
difficult because the only hand-setting sizes in Stempel's
keeping deviate somewhat from their appointed weight
and shape. These differences apparently arose, at least in
part, from restorations and recuttings through the years.
Accordingly, for the new machine-set sizes of the roman
and italic, only those forms were chosen which seemed
particularly characteristic of the Janson original. A re-de-

sign becoming necessary, the Stempel foundry thereupon

also decided to make both missing sizes, the 24 point and 48 point for hand-setting, both in roman and italic. When seven years later the Walbaum roman and italic, in the keeping of the Berthold foundry in Berlin, were taken over for Linotype use in 6 to 12 point sizes, the problems were not much different, since here too a historic face had similarly to be adapted to the requirements of the Linotype system. An unusually interesting work was the 1958 complementing of Trajanus with especially designed Cyrillic characters in display weights of italic and bold.

The tasks the future will bring can hardly diminish. Progress in typography sets ever-new requirements and casts up fresh problems for solution. Above all, the types themselves must be so ordered in the complex technical systems as to lose none of their beauty, for this would mean a backward step in graphic art. The invisible minute labors that lie back of all these things are scarcely suspected by the compositor as he holds his types, or as the machine-compositor regards his matrices. The farther technique advances, the greater become the demands upon the type designer. The counting mechanism of the hot metal composition machines was the problem which had to be solved by the designer in the past. Today we are faced with photocomposition and tomorrow it may be laser composition that makes new pre-suppositions and new demands. The type form must subordinate itself to tech-nical requirements, and be attentive to the increased demands for legibility from the reader; and it remains the type designer's task to be watchful that in modern mass production the letters' beauty be not lost. And the types, designed as a contemporary expression in an in-dustrial society, those types must seek to bring the pur-

(56/57) Working design for the punch-cutter in 36 pt.
Pilot size of the Palatino Italic pasted-up for comparison.

àmbûrgówienystdçp

àmbûrg̊ówienystdçp

HAMBURGEN

YÇX ABDET

zß§e&12345678

zßke & 16.7.1951   5.5.50 *dh*

NG 29.6.49   *k()[]† »*
x   a

HAMBURGEN

ABDETM 24.10.51

1/1

hklxztzchœ!?æffflftfi

iklxztzdiœ!?æffflftfi

PSTKVFQLWZ

RNZÆ,Th ꝫ Œ *Juni 47*

1234567890 ſpſtg

1234567890 *g* ok

" = / ꝫ * - Qu ø *15 3 50* S

PSTKVFQLWZ

Æ,Th * zufett n a e

poseful, the simple and the beautiful into a harmonious

unity. Not in the imitation of the Middle Ages nor in the restoration of the 19th century – though it often looks that way – ought we to seek forms of expression for our day; rather should we satisfy the demands of tomorrow's techniques and thus create types valid as expressions of our time and as a continuance of the tradition of occidental type forms.

The art of the printed book from its revolutionary origin has always welcomed all technical innovations. Gutenberg's invention supplanted the scribes of the Middle Ages, Gutenberg becoming at the same time the trailblazer of modern mass production. Indeed, hand-setting, machine composition and photographic composition are only way-stations of development, all proceeding from his main principle: swiftest production in every desired size of edition.

With all our time-saving, we may one day be like the little prince in the French fairy tale of Antoine de Saint-Exupéry, wherein experts had found that with the most effective thirst-quenching pills fifty-three minutes were saved weekly, since there was no need to go to a well. Whereupon came the little prince's question: How do you use the time so gained? With the time saved us by a photo-composing machine we shall, I suppose (as in Gutenberg's day), in all quiet do a craftsmanlike piece of hand-composition, or simply set a beautifully justified line of foundry type in a composing stick.

Surely there ought to be a Gutenberg monument in Detroit —for Henry Ford should long since have had one erected to the father of modern mass-production. Also, the first Ford cars were all black, and here too I see a somewhat fantastic parallel with Gutenberg's printing, before the lovely bright colors came into use.

In the course of a dinner at the Grolier Club in New York in 1954 I was once asked which of my own types I liked best. A squeamish, awkward question, for what father would openly say which of his daughters he loves best? Naturally he will—where the choice is ample enough— harbor a silent love for one or another. So, I believe Palatino and Melior are not too bad, even if I have exceptional sympathy for Aldus and Optima.

Type is the tie or ligature between author and reader, and it is much to be desired that readers become more critical and gradually more sensitive about the choice of type in a book. In this connection the question arises whether our modern book production shows generally that unity of content and form common, for example, among the books of the 15th and 16th and even later centuries. Why is this unity generally lost? And is it not an anachronism when Albert Einstein's relativity theory, or works by Bertrand Russell, Pasternak and other such are printed with types of historic design? Were the great achievements of book art in the past, too, printed with 'old' types of past epochs? Just think of the books produced in the first decades of printing: of the grand work of Aldus Manutius, *Hypnerotomachia Poliphili,* of the *Theuerdank,* of Charles-Antoine Jombert's *La Fontaine,* and of Bodoni's printings—books, all of them, that rate as typical of the century concerned.

In the 19th century there begins, as in architecture so in books, the imitation of past style epochs—and William Morris himself in the books of the Kelmscott Press gives visible expression to the spell that history had cast upon the 19th century. First in the Doves Press under Cobden-Sanderson the modern contemporary book begins, and is followed in Germany by Walter Tiemann, E. R. Weiss, Rudolf Koch, Paul Renner and F. H. Ernst Schneidler; they created type, and from it books—books that become expressions of our time, books of the 20th century. Books of historical content, books that seek to produce a certain mood or atmosphere in the reader, such books may surely continue to be set in historical or classical types—I do this myself in my own typographic works. On the other hand there are available so many devices expressive of our time that we ought not to banish them when we design books for our time.

The characters and their form should express the spirit of a time, and the artistic background, as for instance do the Roman capitals for the Roman Imperium, the Caroline minuscule and the Textur scripts for the Middle Ages, and then the Renaissance, Baroque and Classicist in their respective printing types.

In 1956 the English Linotype company commissioned me to design a new sans-serif, along with an italic, and a bold with a matching bold italic. Two bold condensed founts were to follow. A rather thankless task, this, because of the abundance of available sans-serif types. I tried a solution that lay midway between the old Grotesk types of the 19th century and the newer versions of the 1930's. Designs for the first trial letters were ready in 1957, the first trial matrices not until 1959. The type was named Magnus.

Attentively I studied Edward Johnston's letters for London Transport dating from 1916, because his serifless roman truly shows proportions of old Roman inscriptions, and not those tedious unexciting letters cast in the middle of the last century, when the main effort was a thorough-going equalization of all the letter-widths, rendering them to a certain degree uniform. In contrast to this is the building up of letter forms on a constructive principle (elements made of straight lines, circles or parts of circles, whereby the widths of the letters result from the corresponding divisions of a square), such as (among others) Rudolf Koch used in his model for the Kabel type in 1926 for Gebr. Klingspor, Offenbach.

I had quiet again in 1957, quiet in which to devote myself to tasks in book design and to typographic plans, since I could concentrate wholly upon my work. There came forth a series of book designs for various publishers; and at the same time I busied myself with the editorial and typographic formation of the second volume of my *Manuale Typographicum* (the first had appeared in 1954 and contained texts concerning type and typography in sixteen different languages).

Naturally I do not use only my own types when I have books to design typographically. Other people too have lovely 'daughters'—as for example the Trump-Mediaeval. It is told of Brahms that when once asked how he liked the Kaiser Waltz of Johann Strauss he replied in honest conviction: »Marvelous! Too bad it's not mine!« Something of the sort happens to me when I look at Roger Excoffon's Mistral type, or my Paris friend Adrian Frutiger's Méridien face, or the Diotima along with its lovely italic by Gudrun Zapf-von Hesse... But this latter 'competitor' has now become less dangerous, for I have married her.

My wife had a bookbinding studio and was a lettering instructor in Frankfurt when I first met her in April of 1948. And here I must insert that in the winter of 1938–39,

I too had worked in a bookbinder's studio which was attached to the Fürsteneck. Even then this noble craft had inspired in me a secret love. But nobody knows how expert a critic I have near me daily, to make me exert myself and so remain doubly attentive to its demands.

An extensive graphic activity began in 1957. I had always greatly delighted in designing publishers' marks (for Insel, S. Fischer, Hanser, Holle, and others). Here, as with type designs, it is often a long pulling and hauling between publisher and artist until there is agreement on a solution. For the Carl Hanser publishing house, for instance, I made over thirty different proposals over a period of four years. Things do not always go so slowly; often the very first version is approved.

The new device of the Carl Hanser Verlag was introduced by Werner Lehmann of Munich on the occasion of the Munich 'Oktoberfest' in 1956 in a spoofing version addressed to the popular taste. Of the three component initials, Lehmann professed to recognize the C as a Munich sausage, the H as the left half of an HB (Hofbräuhaus) beer mug, and the V as made of two bread-sticks— all this surely a Bavarian version of those French ABC games of the 18th and 19th century.

The opportunity came, in 1957 and in the following years, to work out sketches and designs for new types. Such things demand time. The projected purpose of a type determines its form in design. A type contrived for newspaper text will hardly be suited to a volume of lyric verses, any more than an evident advertising face would be for the rendering of a lengthy text. All technical requirements must be considered and regarded even at the drawing stage. An advertising type intended for display purposes can be the spontaneous inspiration of a moment. But a type for book work or for the newspaper rotary press needs a series of considerations, trials and comparisons. Hence a new book- or a newspaper face is the result of months and often years of preparatory work before even the design can first be submitted for approval. Many believe that every drawing of a type that looks in any way interesting is also suited to become a printing type. But

(65) Development of the Hunt Roman. Sketches and first design.
(Was rejected as too narrow)

Buchkunst

Mitglieder *Rough sketches for a German exhibition poster April 1961 Z.*

Hunt Library

Pittsburgh *Early drafts for the Hunt Roman*

ABC abcdefgh

ijklmnopqrst

uvw & xyz *First complete working drawing Oct. 61 too narrow.*

DEGHJMSZ

what is here overlooked is that the written or drawn form,

translated into the typographic, loses in that rigidly-ruled system much of its individuality. Many typographic may-flies passed muster because of this confusion between the original graphic charm of the design as against that achieved through letters shaped by technical needs. A printing face is the sum of a series of factors which must be fused into harmonious unity if a useful type is to re-sult. To be so designed, a type demands of its designer the knowledge of historical coherence in type develop-ment, artistic perception and an inclusive insight into the technique of typecasting.

The type of the future will surely more and more strip away the historic style elements of the past, yet without descending to a geometric-abstract form of letters. For the optical requirements remain the same so long as the letter-images are still received by the human eye and not exclusively by an electronic reading machine. To the tech-

nical requirements in the development of new alphabet

forms, must be added changes in our reading habits.

Until a few years ago, our eye was the only medium which traced the letters. It also was the only judge of good or bad legibility. The artistic aspect was predominant. The eye would discern the less perfect letter design of an alphabet, but, all the same, would finally recognize the meaning of a word or sentence.

Our eye follows, when reading, the upper edge of the middle length (x-height). Attempts to increase this upper »reading line« to improve readability must be taken into consideration when designing readable letterforms in the future, especially alphabets for newspapers, periodicals and text books.

Times for quiet reading have become rare. The large amount of printed text which we have to work through daily compels us to read hastily, a fact that is not always considered. Many of our newspapers and periodicals present hindrances to fluent reading. There is, for example, often a lack of distinction between information, news, and supplementary commentary.

Besides the human eye there is, today, the electronic eye of the reading machines. For these machines, letters are not a problem of form but a problem of distinction, if we wish to keep the amount of reading mistakes low in order to justify the use of these very expensive machines.

Many problems of form have to be taken into consideration for an optical as well as an electronically readable alphabet. Automation in typesetting of large amounts of text will be the task of the technicians; to design readable and formally good alphabets for the coming technical developments in the area of printing is the task of the alphabet designer.

Photocomposition will influence letterforms the same as type casting did with the calligraphy of the medieval monks. For centuries, letterforms were determined by tools and material.

Besides designing types, I was always involved in many other projects and activities. The Carnegie Institute of Technology in Pittsburgh invited me in 1960 for a six-week seminar on lettering and typography as a visiting professor in the College of Fine Arts.

Conscious of working against time, we really used the time, and the students worked hard day and night. The teaching of American students was much different from my experience in Germany and Sweden. The students wanted to know every technical detail, especially time-saving methods and not so much the historical background. It was fascinating to see the progress in so short a period. But I must confess, I learned too, the essentials of our profession and how to explain the possibilities for the future to interested young people.

In 1961 the late Mrs. Rachel McMasters Miller Hunt (1882 to 1963) commissioned me to design a Roman for the

Hunt Botanical Library of Carnegie Institute of Techno-

logy in Pittsburgh. For the first time I had the privilege of

designing a type without any technical restrictions of

units and the like, using the fullest freedom to fix the

proportions of each letter, just as Garamond and Bodoni

had made their types in the golden age of hand compo-

sition. Cut in four sizes from 12 to 24 pt., Hunt Roman

was to be used primarily as a display letter in connection

with the Hunt Botanical Library's existing face, Mono-

type Spectrum, and also as a text-type for special pub-

lications and hand-set publications of limited editions.

Jack Stauffacher and I worked out our ideas about the
form the new type face should take. It took several months
to produce the first sketches of the complete alphabet.
Knowing the special purpose of this new type it was the
idea to design a transitional type that would not take
over the historical particularities of Baskerville or Janson:
I wanted to produce a face that was not a revival but
rather a type of our time.
A special problem arose with the accented letters which
always add to the number of characters in a font. To
reduce the manufacturing costs to a reasonable amount,

I worked out special casting specifications in a somewhat measured system. Normally, separate or piece accents were used above capital letters. This addition of a piece accent was now made also for the lower-case letters, a, e, n, o, and u. A portion of these characters were later cast on a smaller body size, so that the accents could be added to fill the rest of the normal body on the head shoulder. By this unusual method I got a fount of the Hunt Roman of only 90 characters.

The whole story of the design is told in the volume *Hunt Roman: The Birth of a Type,* published in 1965 by the Pittsburgh Bibliophiles. It is edited by George H. M. Lawrence, who played an important part from the very beginning in the whole concept of the Hunt Roman, along with my friend Jack Stauffacher.

From that publication I quote some of the designer's remarks: »Today it is necessary to express the feelings of our times, and the techniques of industrial design, in attempts to conserve or copy historical forms. Although we must respect tradition and the many good inspirations of the past, we should use them thoughtfully to produce things for today's needs. Nor is it possible to express our thoughts and conceptions of the 20th century with types that express the style and therefore the spirit of Renaissance or Colonial periods. Modern thinking should be reflected in books through the selection of typefaces that have been designed according to the modern concepts. The expression of our time should be seen not only in modern architecture, but also in book production and commercial printing. The designer of a new typeface has a responsibility, not only to the past masters of type design–generally speaking, to tradition–but also to the future.«

With the beginning of the 'sixties I had to choose, whether

to confine myself to book typography or to the design

problems of photocomposing. I was stimulated by this

new field and wide scope to the graphic arts which con-

nected my early dreams with my typographical know-

ledge.

More and more the computers force their way into the
printing trade. Problems of alphabet forms will no longer
be solved by the designer alone, by his inspirations and
creativity. The electronics technician will be his comrade
in the future, as in former times was the punch-cutter
for the pilot size of a new type face in a type foundry.
Nevertheless the type-designer—or better, let us start
calling him the alphabet designer—will have to see his
task and his responsibility more than before in the coordination of the tradition in the development of letterforms with the practical purpose and the needs of the
advanced equipment of today.
Things might well be left alone, were it not for all the
new developments now taking place. For example, the
new photocomposing systems using cathode-ray tubes
(CRT) or digital storage for the alphabet—and one day
before very long we will use the laser beam for generat-
ing characters—bring with them some absolutely new
technical problems, many more than did the past with
its solid foundation on historical development in typographic styles.

(72/73) Swash characters of Palatino Italic. First proposals
and working drawings for the punch-cutter.

HOWARD ·

GRÜN · MOZ

TURENNE ·

M · F · WEISE

CHOPIN · FI

KONZERT ·

Okt.
Dez.
1952

A L R U P &

KONZERT

8.10.

ITZ · CHINA
RT · STEMPEL
ETTE & FRY
BIGGO · KID
NZE · GRAZ
ENU · WVAN

M F K H N W

enberger 1. Schnitt
zu leicht, R zu fett

INGR

In the future our work will be governed by analytic ob-

servations on the entire process of manufacturing: by coordination of individual functions down to the last details in contrast with the hit-or-miss methods we still use today, and by carefully planned tests to find the optimal possible solutions for specific typographical tasks (books, magazine, etc.). The typographer will become an analytic designer.

The answer to the coming century of progressive figures will be new methods for storing knowledge, both in forms of books, and by new-style information storage centers, like Micromation, available to everybody.
But also in the future, the book will remain superior to all information stored in a computer, because the book can present instructive details for comparison and especially illustrations in color in a clearly arranged and always visible form.

In provisional summary of my work as book designer the German edition of *Typographic Variations* was published in 1963, the American publication following in 1964 and a French one in 1965.

The volume consists of typographic variations on themes in contemporary book design and typography in 78 book and title pages with prefaces by G. K. Schauer, Paul Standard and Charles Peignot. I still had too many ideas requiring time for experiment. Naturally, I shall design books hereafter, but not as my main job.

I did not wish to enlarge my studio. I only wanted to divide my available time in order to do what I most enjoy. Fortunately, I was able to choose my orders.

In connection with my consulting agreement with Hallmark, and a training program for their lettering artists in Kansas City, the notion came to the Hallmark people of making a film about my work. Originally the film was for the firm's own use, but during its making it was decided to share it with art schools and universities. Entitled *The Art of Hermann Zapf*, the film was made in collaboration with Noel Gordon and Harald Peter, and is now used together with three different permanent Hallmark exhibitions of my work. All these, shown in art schools and clubs, have been traveling since 1968 through the United States and Canada. The film was also shown at the film session of the UNESCO meeting of the Association Typo-

graphique Internationale in Paris 1967.

Our cameraman came from Hawaii. He was used to big outdoor scenes with professional models. It was not easy – but a bottle of whisky helped – to persuade him to shoot only my hands and letters, but finally the idea of the so-called 'frog views' won him over: pictures taken through an astralon-coated glass plate. On this slippery surface I had to write with a broad-edged pen, at midnight, with unpleasantly strong, hot camera lights trained on my neck, and so to design beautiful letters whose ink dried directly as the pen touched the astralon sheet. Really not an easy job and I can now (since this painful experience) understand better why my 'colleagues' in Hollywood have to be paid so well.

Since my 1960 teaching at Carnegie Institute of Techno-logy in Pittsburgh (now Carnegie-Mellon University), I worked on the idea of preparing a book about profes-sional lettering. (During the war I had drafted a manual about the Calligraphic Book, but this was confined to calligraphy and manuscripts.) I feel there is a real need for a guide book to show contemporary possibilities of lettering quite different from what is now usually taught in schools and publications. The first idea was to show

historic examples of lettering and detailed enlargements

together with a synoptical comparison of the cultural

and political background to clarify the development of

letter forms.

But when I heard in 1964 of my friend Erik Lindegren's plan of doing a new book about letters, I dropped the idea and added to his historical examples of alphabets and lettering these new cultural background facts. But space limitations forbade the use of my intended illustrations. In 1967 Hallmark commissioned me to prepare a training program. These Hallmark Lettering Instructions for their lettering artists, worked out with new training methods, unusual tricks and time-saving techniques, are now in exclusive use by Hallmark, Kansas City. They could one day be expanded into a book for self-instruction in a step-by-step method with illustrations in related margins. Such a book, in a simple paperback edition, would not only keep an important tradition alive but also extend its know-how to teach the use of such tools as the brush or the broad-edged pen in building good letter forms in the future.

These instructions and exercises should give a solid basis for useful contemporary lettering. I can only show the way, leaving you to travel at your own pace. If you have a really good foundation, you can always turn back and start again in a new direction if you see yourself going too 'far out'.

Research and studies in letters over several years was the basis for new alphabets. For the exclusive use of Hallmark in Kansas City I designed several alphabets. First came Jeannette in 1967, a script based on American handwriting with many special characters, ligatures, and alternative letters. Firenze, a calligraphic alphabet for film composition was a contemporary version of a Chancery, with additional swash letters. The next was a black letter called Hallmark Textura, which, with its normal small letters, could be used together with an Uncial or the majuscules of the new Shakespeare type.

The latter is a calligraphic Roman (upper and lower case) designed in 1968 for Hallmark by my wife to initiate Hallmark's venture into bookmaking.

For some time now a new avocation—painting—has been added to my professional activities: paintings using various techniques and materials with calligraphic elements and letterforms.

Of course, it is a bit on the abstract side, but not as wild as Pollock nor like Bob Rauschenberg. I want to express my feelings—sometimes a bit pessimistic about the future— in the colors. What I am trying to do is to demonstrate scientific developments, impressions and ideas through the medium of painting. It is more a search for a way to explain and think about important facts—not for amusement—in these days of computers and electronics. Collectors or galleries, you see, will have no chance at all.

People often ask me how I manage all these various jobs in which I am continually engaged. I have two ideal places to work. First my old watch tower in Dreieichenhain ('Three Oaks Grove') near Frankfurt, built in 1460 when Gutenberg was printing the *Catholicon* in Mainz, twenty-five miles away. And my summer place in Cervo, on the Riviera dei Fiori between Genoa and Nice, facing the Mediterranean.

Two places without telephones, two splendid refuges for work. The main question is time, but I think it is much more important how to organize the amount of time given to you within the span of your lifetime. If only we knew our alloted span of days!

In 1968, fourteen years after the publishing of the *Ma-

nuale Typographicum in oblong quarto, the new com-

panion *Manuale* was published in upright format with 100

typographical arrangements with considerations about

types, typography and the art of printing selected from

past and present, printed in eighteen languages. This

time it was not printed in the private printing office of

the Stempel Foundry. I managed the book on my own

and it was an enormous financial burden.

As I had to be its publisher, I founded the Z-Press. Not only the troubles of a publisher but a lot of tax problems arose besides bookkeeping, mailing and shipping, storage and organizing the whole. From the beginning of this new book I could not imagine what it would mean to select and to check 118 texts in 18 languages and to work with many composing rooms in the various countries. The first *Manuale* was exclusively composed from types of the Stempel Foundry in Frankfurt. The new book includes 90 different faces from all over the world, hand composition, Monotype, Linotype and photocomposition. There were arguments with customs people when receiving copper shells for electros or lead from East-European countries. Sometimes I had the feeling they thought I was handling strategic materials. Who invented bureaucracy?
The book thus shows the newly extended range of typo-

(81) Redesign of Melior Roman for use in photocomposition,
with notes and explanations for new designs.

graphy, since photocomposition will succeed the era of 'classical typography' and will thus user in the future.

82 From its preface I quote some lines about the background of this publication: »It was delight—a delight in working with type, in shaping and finding fresh means of expression, that, after years of work, brought the *Manuale Typographicum* into being. It is a printed record of letters at play, involving effort and labor which only the expert will perceive. May it bring, for many others, access to the world of type and typography and to their great wealth of letterforms.«

»The polyglot texts show that people have long been, and still are, concerned with the problems of type, of printing and of bookmaking. Even in the electronic age these problems have not lost their significance, particularly since their technical development steadily assigns special tasks to printing. Novel possibilities in photocomposition bring many alterations in its output. Typographers and type-designers too must adapt themselves to these conditions, and yet the fundamentals of typography remain basically unchanged.«

Since childhood, I have had a special liking for electrical engineering. Everything connected with this caught my interest. The only problem I had in all those years was to find the time requisite to such studies, since more and more I was absorbed by my professional work as a graphic designer.

Electronics was not yet known in those days of my school-time, nor the effect of bimetallic platings which is today so important in the field of automation. I developed an automatic coffee-machine in 1933. It looked more like a combination of a motor car's engine and an infernal machine, without any notion of shaping my construction, a quality now conferred by industrial design.

But the general knowledge is now very useful in my work on photocomposing systems and computerized composition. Before the technicians do everything and even design the letters, I think it better for me to attempt an act of deliverance, especially (as also may be possible one day) since letters themselves may finally be produced directly from the computer, and this exclusively from the scanning of the reading machine (OCR). Even today the digital pre-programmed structure permits manipulation from a basic alphabet into an italic with bold, condensed or expanded versions. For years I have studied and analyzed an alphabet to be based on a pure logical concept completely under digital control.

It is a rare good fortune, surely, if the handsome alphabets of a designer come into some measure of agreement with the calm considerations of the type-founders or firms producing photocomposing systems, or, above all, the sales managers. The one sees only his letters for whose sake he has so long plagued himself, whereas the other side surveys reflectively the state of the market. Can it be that 'sales people' are chiefly interested in the figures 1 to 0 – and even then in a suitable composition – and perhaps rather less in the actual letters A–Z?

Type designers have tasks enough even in this age of electronic miraclemachines; and photosetting will see to it that the last third of the 20th century too will be interesting for us. For every photocomposition system creates new problems, if the alphabet is generated by a cathode-ray tube or digitally stored in a magnetic memory—or in the near future shaped by a laser beam. They all will still need alphabets; and to collaborate in this will provide much interest in the future to a plain alphabet designer. The very prospect must stimulate every working designer.

It was necessary to devote more and more time for basic

research and to establish my own archive for computer-

ized composition and for publications connected with

alphabets generated by cathode-ray tube and with com-

puter typesetting. I always wanted to have everything at

hand to work out analytic composition programs for com-

plex printing jobs and future studies.

Here I should mention the program for automatic spacing for a firm specializing in photocomposition in Kansas City, which was drafted for an IBM 1130 in connection with a Linofilm.
I figured out a system based on additional small units for all possible letter combinations to space automatically words in capital letters. It is possible to use this program for various type faces with just a few changes for especially difficult characters.
For the first time, in 1964, in a lecture at the Carpenter

Center of Harvard University, and again in 1969 in Prague during the congress of the Association Typographique Internationale on »Typographic Opportunities in the Com- puter Age,« I presented design problems in connection with photocomposition and discussed the outlook for future developments saying: »I think there is no question that we have to create a new concept in the typographic field. This indicates the common trend which is part of our present day and future way of living. There is a permanent movement in so many fields towards the future. We too often look backwards in our love for the old-timers in types; we are sometimes still captured by false romanticism, and we should spend part of our activities for new developments.«

»We need new concepts, not historical copies. Photocomposition offers so many new possibilities: so far the letter form has been static and could be controlled every time. But now, photocomposition can change all forms like rubber. Computerized composition with pre-programmed details needs a new thinking in terms of phototypography. Today it is possible to produce complete books by computers. All the data are directly supplied from the computer into ultra-high-speed photocomposing machines. The make-up is pre-programmed. Without photocomposition, that is by conventional means, such jobs could never be handled with such speed. Our possibilities as book designers and our imagination are not capable of estimating or outdoing the capacity of an electronic computer. And just this enormous variety of possibilities, on the other hand, leads us to new thoughts, new considerations.«

I see a vast task for designers if we are to cope with increasing world population (even today we have 750 million illiterates despite computers and moon landings) and with the increase in sciences and technologies (their literatures doubling within every decade).

Of a useful text type created by the purpose of our time, more is asked today than that it be only a readily legible book type. There are no universal types suited to every use, since the many different printing processes render that impossible. We should all be satisfied that so splendid an armory of printing types is available for these tasks. Alongside the tried and tested classical faces, however, the efforts for a form true to our time also have their justification, since they must often serve the requirements of the modern printing processes, to which indeed they owe their origin.

Few who daily read the printed word ever consider how those component letters came to be. Yet every single letter of our alphabet has been shaped by the constant effort to render its image suitable in purpose and beautiful in form. It is not only the designer of a type face who creates the form of its letters: many hands join in the common task to find the final and the best adaptation of the creative artist's design. Rarely has there been an activity with consequences so manifold and far-reaching as those of the formation of a printing type. Those engaged in this work have thus incurred a great responsibility; they take satisfaction in knowing that their work may represent one of the most noble and progressive of all human activities.

And if letters, 'our' letters, were to help only once to lessen hatred and mistrust among peoples; if the many printed reports were to make a dweller on this earth into the happiest being, if printed letters might once rout a calumny with truth, or through a consoling book reconcile a single human being with his fellow-creatures, then shall we be immune against all the glitter of riches, the lust for power and idle fame, which seduce so many. If the letters daily produced by the millions in the printing presses were to be used for only one good purpose every day, then—despite all abuse—all the pains we have taken with their creation will have been rewarded.

(88/89) Drawing for the Sistina capitals with instructions
for the cutting by hand.

EFM
Kontur nicht

YZU ?U

PSV
V?

TBXN

VKRI

W?

ARL

Pandora
Sistina

*

LTG!

*

CJQ

?Q

Z.

WRITINGS AND PUBLICATIONS BY HZ

(in books and periodicals up to September 1969)

Das Vermächtnis von Rudolf Koch. *Nürnberger Hefte. Monatsschrift für Kunst und geistiges Leben in Franken.* Vol. I, No. 4. Nürnberg: Nürnberger Presse. April 1949. pp. 12–17. With 2 illustrations.

Friedrich Wilhelm Kleukens. *Der Druckspiegel.* Vol. III, No. 8. Stuttgart August 1948. pp. 18–19. With 2 illustr.

Das Blumen-ABC von Hermann Zapf und August Rosenberger. Frankfurt a. M.: Privately printed for Hermann Zapf 1949. 4to. With 28 illustrations.

William Morris. Sein Leben und Werk in der Geschichte der Buch- und Schriftkunst. Monographien künstlerischer Schrift. Vol. XI. Scharbeutz: Klaus Blanckertz 1949. 4to. With 36 illustrations and frontispiece.

Feder und Stichel. Alphabete und Schriftblätter in zeitgemäßer Darstellung. Frankfurt a. M.: D. Stempel AG 1950. Oblong 4to. With 25 plates.

Zur Stilgeschichte der Druckschriften. *Imprimatur.* Vol. X, MCML-MCMLI (Hamburg): Gesellschaft der Bibliophilen 1951. pp. 83–108. With 43 illustrations.

Feder und Stichel. Alphabete und Schriftblätter, geschrieben von Hermann Zapf, in Metall geschnitten von August Rosenberger. Fourth publication Trajanus-Presse. Frankfurt a. M. 1952. Oblong 4to. With 25 plates.

Pen and Graver. Alphabets and Pages of Calligraphy by Hermann Zapf with a Preface by Paul Standard. New York: Museum Books 1952. Oblong 4to. With 25 plates.

Introduction to Paul Koch *Notenschreibbüchlein.* Second edition. Wolfenbüttel: Karl Heinrich Möseler 1953.

Gift med Bogstaverne. *De Grafiske Fag.* No. 3. Copenhagen 1953. pp. 194–195.

Vom Formgesetz der Renaissance-Antiqua. *Gutenberg-Jahrbuch 1953.* Mainz 1953. pp. 11–15. With 8 illustr.

Zur Klassifizierung der Druckschriften. *Form und Technik.* Vol. IV, No. 9. Stuttgart Sept. 1953. p. 340.

Manuale Typographicum. German edition Frankfurt a. M.: Georg Kurt Schauer 1954. American edition: New York: Museum Books 1954. Oblong 4to. 100 typographic pages with quotations from the past and present on types and printing in sixteen different languages, selected and designed by Hermann Zapf. Printed at the house printing-office of the Stempel type-foundry, Frankfurt a. M., with an afterword by Paul Standard, New York. (With a supplement of translations)

Die Stilgruppen der Antiqua und ihre charakteristischen Elemente. *Gutenberg-Jahrbuch 1954.* Mainz 1954. pp. 9–15. With 1 plate.

Buchstabenverformungen seit der Renaissance. *Folium* III, 3–4. Utrecht: H. L. Gumbert 1954. pp. 92–96. With 4 illustrations.

Gedanken zur heutigen Situation der Typographie. *Gutenberg-Jahrbuch 1956*. Mainz 1956. pp. 368–373. With 4 illustrations.

Are You Still Driving an 1890 Model Car? *Inspired Typography '66*. New York: The Type Directors Club 1956. [pp. 13–14]

Kleine Autobiographie in Lettern. *Der Druckspiegel* Vol. XI, No. 11. Stuttgart November 1956 [16 pages]. With 45 illustrations.

Die Wechselbeziehungen von Handschrift und Drucktype. *Imprimatur. Ein Jahrbuch für Bücherfreunde.* New Series, Vol. I, 1956/1957. Frankfurt a. M.: Gesellschaft der Bibliophilen 1957. pp. 150–157. With 9 illustrations.

Gedanken und Probleme beim Entwurf von Werkschriften. *Philobiblon. Eine Vierteljahresschrift für Buch- und Graphik-Sammler.* Vol. II, No. 4. Hamburg: Dr. Ernst Hauswedell. November 1958. pp. 315–330. Illustrated.

Cooperation of Many Hands Shapes Our Letters. *Letters and Nils Larson. Reflections on His Contributions to Typographical Development 1922–1959. Brooklyn,* New York: Mergenthaler Linotype Company 1959. pp. 14–15. (Privately printed)

Autobiography in Type. *Motif 3*. London: The Shenval Press. Sept. 1959. pp. 33–48. With 49 illustrations.

Zur Klassifizierung der Druckschriften. *Der Druckspiegel.* Vol. XIV, No. 12. Stuttgart Dezember 1959. pp. 611–614.

Zur Pflege der Schreibkunst. *Imprimatur.* New Series, Vol. II. Frankfurt a. M. 1958/1959. pp. 220–221. With 7 illustrations.

Über Alphabete. Gedanken und Anmerkungen beim Schriftentwerfen. Frankfurt a. M. 1960. 120 pages. With 12 illustrations and 24 type specimens.

About Alphabets. Some marginal Notes on Type Design. New York. The Typophiles, 1960. 120 pages. With 12 illustrations and 24 type specimens.

In memoriam Oldřicha Menharta. *Typografia.* Prague 1962. No. 5. p. 12.

Gutenberg kontra Dali. *Graphic.* Vol. III. Brussels. September 1962. pp. 3–7. In French (translated by Berthe Delépinne) and in German.

Schrifttypen und Bücher als Ausdruck ihrer Zeit. Gedanken über grundsätzliche Fragen der Buchtypographie in der Gegenwart. *Gutenberg-Jahrbuch 1962.* Mainz 1962. pp. 68–75. With 7 illustrations.

Printing types and books: An expression of their times: *The Penrose Annual.* Vol. 36. London 1962. pp. 47–53.

Typographische Variationen. 78 Buchtitel und Textseiten als Gestaltungsmöglichkeiten der Typographie und Buchgraphik. Prefaces by G. K. Schauer, Frankfurt am Main; Paul Standard, New York and Charles Peignot, Paris. German edition Frankfurt am Main 1963. English edition New York 1964. French edition Paris 1965. 168 pages.

La typographie du livre moderne, répond-elle au style qui représente notre époque? *Caractère Noel.* Images et Imagination, Chapitre 5. Paris 1963. 8 pages. With 20 illustrations.

Designing of a Type Face for the Book in the 1960's. *Format.* Published by the Society of Typographic Designers of Canada. Toronto October 1964. With 6 illustrations.

The Meaning of Modern. *Print.* New York September/October 1964. pp. 27–29. With 4 illustrations.

Hunt Roman: The Birth of a Type. Commentary and Notes by Hermann Zapf and Jack Stauffacher. Foreword by George H. M. Lawrence. The Pittsburgh Bibliophiles. Pittsburgh 1965. pp. 19–24. With 11 illustrations.

Schriftgestaltung, Typographie, Photosatz und automatische Satzherstellung. *Deutscher Drucker.* No. 11. Stuttgart 7 April 1965. p. 5.

Vom Felsbild zum Alphabet. Die Geschichte der Schrift von ihren frühesten Vorstufen bis zur modernen lateinischen Schreibschrift. *Deutscher Drucker.* No. 4. Stuttgart 26 January 1967. pp. 9–13. With 4 illustrations.

Incidence de l'évolution des techniques sur le dessin des caractères. (UNESCO, 9 November 1967.) *Techniques graphiques.* No. 73, 11/12. Paris 1967. pp. 771–782. With 7 illustrations.

Die Probleme der Typographie in der Zukunft. *Gutenberg-Jahrbuch 1968.* Mainz 1968. pp. 35–39. With 3 illustr.

Das neue Manuale Typographicum. Ein Bericht über 14 Jahre. *Philobiblon*. Vol. 12. No. 4. Hamburg 1968. With 8 illustrations.

Adrian Frutiger. Introduction for the type specimen of *Serifa*. Bauersche Gießerei, Frankfurt a. M. 1968. p. 4.

The many faces of Zapf. *Lithopinion*. Vol. 3. No. 2. Issue 10. New York 1968. pp. 57–65. With 14 illustrations.

Die Veränderung der Schriftform durch die technische Entwicklung. *Polygraph Jahrbuch 1968*. Frankfurt a. M. 1968. pp. 1–11. With 12 illustrations.

Phototypography Offers Challenge. *Printing News*. New York 18 May 1968. pp. 10–16.

Book Design in the Past and Future. *Homage to the Book*. Westvaco 1968. New York. pp. 1–4. With 2 illustrations.

The Changes in Letterforms Due to Technical Developments. *The Journal of Typographic Research*. Vol. II. Cleveland 1968. pp. 351–368. With illustrations.

Problemy projektowania pism dziełowych. *Litera*. Warszawa. Rok III. No. 21–3, 1968. pp. 41–43 (1 illustration); No. 23–5, 1968. pp. 78–80 (1 illustration); No. 24–6, 1968, pp. 94–96 (3 illustrations).

Manuale Typographicum. 100 typographische Gestaltungen mit Aussagen über die Schrift, über Typographie und Druckkunst, aus Vergangenheit und Gegenwart, in achtzehn verschiedenen Sprachen. 100 typographical arrangements with considerations about types, typography and the art of printing selected from past and present, printed in eighteen languages. Z-Presse. Frankfurt–New York. Museum Books New York 1968. 242 pages.

Veränderungen der Schriftformen durch die technische Entwicklung. *Typografie*. Vol. 18. No. 1. Leipzig January 1969. pp. 11–16. With 6 illustrations.

Att planera för framtiden. *Grafiska Institutet Tjugofem år*. Stockholm 1969. pp. 33–35. With 1 illustration.

Konec klasické typografie a příchod doby progresívních čísel. *Grafotechna*. Prague 1969. pp. 1–6. With 5 illustr.

Analphabeten in Deutschland. Kritische Betrachtungen zu öffentlichen Beschriftungen. *Werk und Zeit*. Vol. 18. No. 8. Düsseldorf August 1969. p. 4. With 4 illustrations.

Die klassische Typographie und die Photosatz-Programme von morgen. *Gutenberg-Jahrbuch 1969*. Mainz 1969. pp. 29–31.

(97) Page from *Typographic Variations*. Title page arrangement of different plays together with the page-figures.

Amerikanisches Theater

4 Theaterstücke

Mit einem Nachwort von S. Melchinger

Büchergilde Gutenberg Frankfurt/Main

98   Schmoller, Hans P.: Engraved Calligraphy. *Signature*. New Series No. 13. London 1951. pp. 61–62. With 2 illustr.

Hack, Bertold: Palatino, eine neue Schrift der Schriftgießerei D. Stempel AG. *Börsenblatt für den Deutschen Buchhandel,* Frankfurt a. M. No. 72, 7 Sept. 1951. pp. 309–311.

Standard, Paul: Hermann Zapf. At 32 he is Known as one of the Finest of Calligraphers. *American Printer.* Vol. 133, No. 1. New York Jan. 1952. pp. 20–21 and 64–65. With 2 illustrations.

Zachrisson, Bror: Handens mästare. *Grafisk Forum.* Vol. 57, No. 2. Stockholm Febr. 1952. pp. 55–57. With 3 illustr.

Falk, Valter: Hermann Zapf. Ung tysk bokstavskonstnär i Världsklass. *Nordisk Boktryckarekonst.* Vol. 53, No. 4. Stockholm: Sten Lagerström April 1952. pp. 107–110. With 4 illustrations.

Berg, Yngve: Mästare i skriftkonst. *Dagens Nyheter.* Stockholm 29 May 1952. p. 4. With 2 illustrations.

Schauer, Georg Kurt: Feder und Stichel. Ein Gang zu den Quellen der Druckschrift. *Der Druckspiegel.* Vol. VIII, No. 7. Stuttgart July 1953. pp. 354–360. With 6 illustr.

Hölscher, Eberhard: Hermann Zapf. Manuale Typographicum. *Gebrauchsgraphik.* Vol. XXVI, No. 10. München: F. Bruckmann KG. October 1955. pp. 42–49. With 13 illustrations.

Rodenberg, Julius and Schauer, Georg Kurt: Schrift als Bild. Betrachtungen zum Manuale Typographicum von Hermann Zapf. *Der Druckspiegel*. Vol.X, No.11. Stuttgart 1955. 8 pages. With 3 illustrations.

Moran, James: A Humanizing Experience. Zapf's Manuale Typographicum. *Printing News*. London 22 March 1956. p.4. With 4 illustrations.

Sedláček, František: Manuale Typographicum. *Typografia*. No.8. Praha 1956. 6 pages. With 12 illustrations.

Souček, Stanislav: Abecedy a psané listy v dobovém podání, Pero a Rýtko. Napsal Hermann Zapf – Do kovu vyryl August Rosenberger (Frankfurt am Main). *Typografia*. No.8. Praha 1956. 2 pages. With 4 illustrations.

Ohchi, Hiroshi: Hermann Zapf. *Idea*. Vol.5, No.30. Tokyo: Seibundo-Shinkosha Publishing Co. Aug.1958. pp. 20–29. With 45 illustrations.

Szántó, Tibor: Hermann Zapf. Manuale Typographicum. *Magyar Grafika*. Budapest: Müszaki Könyvkiadó 1959. pp.19–26. With 14 illustrations.

Schauer, Georg Kurt: Hermann Zapf, Calligrapher and Book Designer, Frankfurt/Main (Germany). *Book Design and Production*. Vol.2, No.4. London: Printing News 1959. pp.25–32. With 18 illustrations.

Schmoller, Hans P.: Hermann Zapf, Type Designer. *Motif 3*. London: The Shenval Press Sept.1959. pp.49–50. With 1 illustration.

Eikeren, Joh. van: Geschriften van Hermann Zapf. *Drukkersweekblad.* Vol. 47, No. 39. Amsterdam 26 September 1959, pp. 926–927. With 1 illustration.

Lawson, Alexander: Hermann Zapf, Major Contemporary Designer. *Inland Printer and American Lithographer.* Chicago July 1960. pp. 82–83. With 2 illustrations.

Martin, Noel: Hermann Zapf, Calligrapher–Type Designer–Typographer. *Carnegie Magazine.* Pittsburgh October 1960, pp. 277–279.

McBrinn, Seán: Hermann Zapf, Calligrapher–Book Designer. *Modern Irish Printer.* Vol. 2. No. 3. Dublin. Winter 1960/61. pp. 21–28. With 16 illustrations.

Standard, Paul: Hermann Zapf in Amerika. Betrachtungen zu einer Ausstellungsfolge. *Börsenblatt für den Deutschen Buchhandel.* Frankfurt a. M. 13 January 1961. pp. 49–51.

Hermann Zapf's Autobiography in Letters. *Productionwise.* No. 1. New York 1961. pp. 52–54. With 1 illustration.

Hermann Zapf. Weg und Werk des Frankfurter Schriftgestalters. *Frankfurt. Lebendige Stadt.* Vol. 2, 1961. pp. 54–57.

Speckter, Martin K.: The Versatile Mr. Zapf. *Type Talks.* No. 116. New York March/April 1961. pp. 10–12. With 3 illustrations.

Bloem, Wim: Hermann Zapf. *Mahez News.* Vol. 7. Amsterdam May 1961. 4 pages. With 15 illustrations.

Lyman, Nanci: Hermann Zapf, Type Designer and Calligrapher. *Print*. Vol. 15. No. 2. New York March/April 1961. pp. 44–49. With 15 illustrations.

Fischerström, Iwan W.: Självbiografiskt av Hermann Zapf. *Nordisk Boktryckarekonst*. Vol. 62. No. 4. Stockholm 1961. pp. 128–130. With 4 illustrations.

Dooijes, Dick: Een pleidooi voor het gebruik van eigentijdse lettervormen. (Langs de weg geplukt). *Drukkersweekblad*. Vol. 49. No. 16. Amsterdam 21 April 1961. pp. 434–435. With 1 illustration.

Souček, Stanislav: Abecedy Hermanna Zapfa. *Typografia*. Prague 1961. No. 6/7. 19 pages. With 37 illustrations.

Ellegaard Frederiksen, Erik: Der er andre problemer end de teknisk-faglige. *De grafiske. Fag*. No. 9. Copenhagen September 1961. pp. 294–296. With 2 illustrations.

Rohde, Bent: Hermann Zapf. Somgæsteforelæser pa Den Grafiske Højskole. *De grafiske Fag*. Copenhagen March 1962. No. 3. p. 115. With 1 illustration.

Weidemann, Kurt: Schrift und Typographie im Buch. In: *Der Druckspiegel*. Stuttgart March 1962. Vol. 17. No. 3. 16 pages. With 30 illustrations.

Weidemann, Kurt: Hermann Zapf. Designer's Profile. *Print in Britain*. London January 1963. pp. 29–34. With 22 illustr.

Primera versión alemana de la Divina Proporción Tipográfica de Rosarivo. In: *Argentina Grafica*. Año XXVIII. No. 208.

Buenos Aires January/February/March 1963. 2 pages. With 2 illustrations. (Preface of the German edition in Spanish.)

Zirnbauer, H.: Rudolf Koch und Hermann Zapf. Ausstellung in der Stadtbibliothek Nürnberg, Februar bis April 1963. *Börsenblatt für den Deutschen Buchhandel*. Frankfurter Ausgabe. No. 26. March 1963. pp. 528–530.

Hermann Zapf in Paris. *Börsenblatt für den Deutschen Buchhandel*. Frankfurt a. M. No. 44. May 1963. pp. 984–985.

Master-Printer. Typographic Variations. Designed by Hermann Zapf on themes in contemporary book design and typography in seventy-eight book and title pages. Limited edition. New York: Museum Books. *The Times Literary Supplement*. London Thursday, 13 August 1964.

Johnson, Fridolf: Hermann Zapf's Letters. *American Artist*. Vol. 28. No. 8. Stamford, Conn., October 1964. pp. 42–47 and 65–66. With 12 illustrations.

Bennett, Paul A.: Hermann Zapf: Calligrapher, Type Designer, Master of the Book Arts. *Publishers' Weekly*. Vol. 187. No. 1. New York 4 January 1965. pp. 72–85. With 6 illustrations.

Schauer, Georg Kurt: Anruf und Selbstbenennung. (Über das Buch Typographische Variationen.) *Polygraph Jahrbuch 1965*. Frankfurt a. M. 1965. pp. 29–39. With 11 illustrations.

Type Designing for Tomorrow. (Gekürzte Übersetzung eines Vortrages von Hermann Zapf über Schriftgestaltung in der Zukunft, gehalten am 27. Oktober 1964 an der Harvard University.) *Linotype-Post.* No. 63. Frankfurt a. M. and Berlin. April 1965. pp. 21–22.

Souček, Stanislav: Hermann Zapf. *Typografia.* Prague September 1965. No. 9. pp. 1–14. With 17 illustrations.

Šulc, Dušan: Neobvyklá Výstava. *Slovenské pohľady.* Bratislava 1965. No. 12. pp. 147–148.

Gardner, Arthur E.: Hermann Zapf Programmed Typographics. *CIS-Newsletter.* Los Angeles 15 December 1965. pp. 1–2. With 1 illustration.

Lawson, Alexander: Hunt Roman. A Private Type by Hermann Zapf. *Inland Printer and American Lithographer.* Chicago April 1966. pp. 82–83. With 3 illustrations.

Weidemann, Kurt: Hermann Zapf. *Typografia.* Prague 1966. No. 8. pp. 169–180. With 35 illustrations.

Gammelmark, Albert: Vor tids skrifttegnere Hermann Zapf. *Vort medlemsblad.* Vol. 44. No. 10. Copenhagen 10 October 1966. pp. 4–9. With 8 illustrations.

Gammelmark, Albert: Vår tids skrifttegnere: Hermann Zapf. *Norsk faktortidende.* Vol. 44. No. 6. Oslo June 1967 pp. 192–194. With 5 illustrations.

Benešová, Bojka and Drbohlav, Vladimír: Hovoři Hermann Zapf. *Typografia.* Prague 1967. No. 9. p. 263. With 1 illustr.

Gammelmark, Albert: Vor tids skrifttegnere: Hermann

(104/105) Calligraphic broadside with classical Roman capitals and quotations in English, French, Greek, and German.

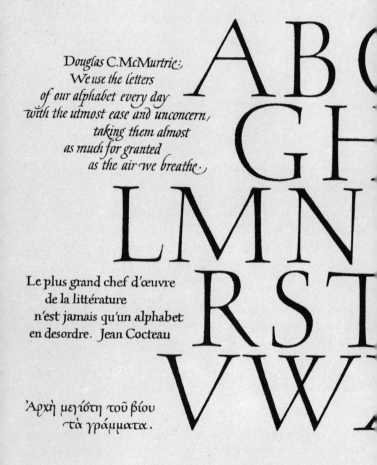

Douglas C. McMurtrie:
We use the letters
of our alphabet every day
with the utmost ease and unconcern,
taking them almost
as much for granted
as the air we breathe.

Le plus grand chef d'œuvre
de la littérature
n'est jamais qu'un alphabet
en desordre. Jean Cocteau

Ἀρχὴ μεγίστη τοῦ βίου
τὰ γράμματα.

ABC
GH
LMN
RST
VW

DEF
JK
PQ
J

We do not realize that each
of these letters is at our service today
only as the result of a long
and laboriously slow process of evolution
in the age-old art
of writing.

YZ

Das größeste
ist das Alphabet,
denn alle Weisheit steckt darin.
Aber nur der erkennt den Sinn, der's recht
zusammenzusetzen
versteht.
Emanuel Geibel

Hermann Zapf

Zapf. *Typograf-Tidende.* Vol. 94. No. 47. Copenhagen 24 November 1967. pp. 412–414. With 5 illustrations.

Lazurski, V. V.: The book and type designer Hermann Zapf. *The Art of the Book 1961–1962.* Moscow 1967. pp. 138–152. With 20 illustrations.

Johnson, William: H. Z. A Portrait of the Artist. *Cards.* Kansas City/Missouri. Spring 1968. pp. 8–11. With 4 illustr.

Filby, P. W.: Hermann Zapf. Manuale Typographicum. *Library Journal.* New York 17 June 1968. p. 2641.

Ubeda, A. G.: Hermann Zapf, acaba de publicar su Manuale Typographicum, una obra maestra de la tipografía europea. *Graficas.* No. 7–8. Madrid 1968. p. 674.

Tomaszewski, Roman: ATYPI-kongres wspołpracy. *Litera.* Warszawa. Rok. III. No. 25–7, 1968. pp. 108–112. With 4 illustrations.

Meuer, Adolph: Ein Compendium der Typographie. *Der Druckspiegel.* Stuttgart October 1968. pp. 58–60. With 2 illustrations.

Rapp, Hermann: Hermann Zapf zum 50. Geburtstag. *Der Polygraph.* Vol. 21. No. 21. Frankfurt a. M. 5 November 1968. 4 pages. With 8 illustrations.

Trump, Georg: Wie man mit 80 Schriftcharakteren zaubern kann. Ein neues Manuale Typographicum von Hermann Zapf. *Deutscher Drucker.* Stuttgart 19 December 1968. p. XIII.

Ovink, G. W.: Hermann Zapf, een typograaf die is, zoals hij is: zichzelf. *Drukkersweekblad*. Vol. 56. No. 51. Amsterdam 27 Dec. 1968. pp. 1374–1375. With 3 illustr.

Walkate, H.: Typografie: communicatie bij uitstek. *Het Vaderland*. The Hague 4 January 1969. p. 5. With 1 illustr.

Gammelmark, Albert: Fornem typografisk håndbog. *Vort Medlemsblad*. Vol. 47. No. 4. Copenhagen 15 April 1969. p. 17. With 2 illustrations.

Modini, Albert: Exposition Hermann Zapf. Calligraphie-typographie, de la main à l'ordinateur. *Nice-Matin*. No. 7843. Nice 11 May 1969.

Raymond, Don Stirling: Zapf Views Changes in Type Design As Result of Impact of Photosetting. *Printing News*. Vol. LXXXIII, No. 5. New York 2 August 1969. pp. 1, 21 and 26. With 3 illustrations.

Meuer, Adolph: A. TYP. I. und das Schriftbild in der Öffentlichkeit. Der Computer in der Druckerei. *Druck–Print*. No. 8, 1969. pp. 659–660.

Standard, Paul and Chandler B. Grannis: Zapf on Type Design for Today and Tomorrow. *Publishers' Weekly*. Vol. 196. No. 5. New York 4 August 1969. pp. 61–63. With 6 illustrations.

Letters at play. Hermann Zapf: Manuale Typographicum. *The Times Literary Supplement*. London Thursday, 25 September 1969. p. 1111.

TYPE SPECIMENS

108   D. Stempel AG and Linotype GmbH, Frankfurt am Main
       Mergenthaler Linotype Company, Plainview/New York
       Hunt Botanical Library, Carnegie-Mellon University,
       Pittsburgh
       Hallmark Cards, Inc. Kansas City/Missouri

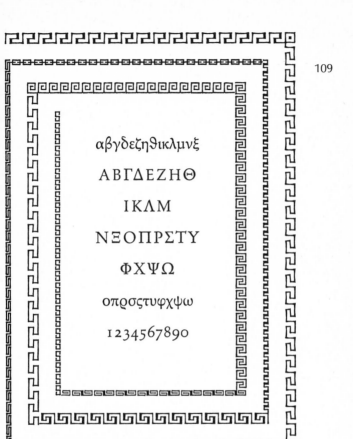

αβγδεζηϑικλμνξ

ΑΒΓΔΕΖΗΘ

ΙΚΛΜ

ΝΞΟΠΡΣΤΥ

ΦΧΨΩ

οπϱϛτυφχψω

1234567890

Attika Borders / Heraklit Greek

Gilgengart I ABCDOEFG

HIIKLLMNOPQRSTUVWXYZ

abcdefghijklmnopqrſstuvwxyzſiſſſtßttz

¢abcdefghijklmnop
qrſstuvwxyzchſtßzghy⸺ſ⸺t

⸺⸺k⸺⸺
ABCDEFGHIIKLM
NOPQRSTUVWXYZ

Gilgengart II ABCDEFG

HIIKLMNOPQRSTUVWXYZ

abcdefghijklmnopqrſstuvwxyz1234567890

Gilgengart (first trial and final form)

𝔄𝔅ℭ𝔇𝔈𝔉𝔊𝔥𝔍
𝔍𝔎𝔏𝔐𝔑𝔒𝔓𝔔𝔔ℜ
𝔖𝔗𝔘𝔙𝔚𝔛𝔜𝔷𝔷

abcdefghijklmnopqrstuvwxyz & æœç 1234567890

ABCDEFGHIJKLMNOPQRSTUVWXYZÆŒ

abcdefghijklmnopqrstuvwxyz & æœç 1234567890

ABCDEFGHIJKLMNOPQRSTUVWXYZÆŒ

abcdefghijklmnopqrstuvwxyz æœç 1234567890

ABCDEFGHIJKLMNOPQRSTUVWXYZ

Gilgengart Initials / Novalis (experimental characters)

abcdefgh
ijklmnopqrstuvwxyzßtz
1234567890

ABCDEFGHI
JKLMNOPQRSTUV
WXYZ & Qu

The art of printing, which diffuses so general a light,

augmenting with the growing day, and of so

penetrating a nature, that all the window shutters,

which despotism and priestcraft can oppose

to keep it out, prove insufficient. *Benjamin Franklin*

Palatino

abcdefghijklmnopqrstuvwxyz

ABCDEFGHIJKLMNOPQRSTUVWXYZ

1234567890

abcdefghijklmnopqrstuvwxyz

ABCDEFGHIJKLMNOPQRSTUVWXYZ

1234567890

Aus reiner Anschauungslust darüber nachzusinnen,

wieviel tüchtigen Händen und Köpfen das

Zustandekommen eines einzigen schönen Buchstabens zu

verdanken ist, das weckt mehr Gemeinschaftsgefühl

als aller Redestreit der Weltverbesserer. *Richard Dehmel*

Linotype Aldus and Italic

abcdefghijklm
nopqrstuvwxyz(pqsvwy)
1234567890

ABCDEFG
HIJKLMNOPQRST
UVWXYZ(EFS)

☉ ☿ ♀ ⊕ ♂ ♃ ♄ ⛢ ♆ ♇ ⚵ ⚶ ⚷

♈ ♉ ♊ ♋ ♌ ♍ ♎ ♏ ♐ ♑ ♒ ♓ ☽

Le plus grand chef-d'œuvre de la littérature n'est jamais

qu'un alphabet en désordre. Jean Cocteau

Palatino, alternative characters / Zodiac Signs

abcdefghijklm
nopqrstuvwxyzfffififlftßtzttkze
1234567890

ABCDEFGH
IJKLMNOPQRSTU
VWXYZ&Qu

ABCDEFG
HIJKLMNOPQR
STUVWXYZ
&
AMNRSTh

Palatino Italic with Swash Characters

ABCDEFGHI
JKLMNOPQRST
UVWXY&Z
KQRS
[1234567890]

*

ΑΒΓΔΕΖΗΘΙ
ΚΛΜΝΞΟΠΡΣΤΥ
ΦΧΨΩ

☩

ΑΡΧΗ ΜΕΓΙΣΤΗ
ΤΟΥ ΒΙΟΥ
ΤΑ ΓΡΑΜΜΑΤΑ

Michelangelo Titling and Phidias Greek

ABCDEFGH
IJKLMNOPQRSTU
VWXYZ✝
&
1234567890
LQRT

---

abcdefghijkl
mnopqrstuvwxyz ttß
&
ABCDEFGH
IJKLMNOPQRSTU
VWXYZ

Sistina Titling / Brush Borders / Palatino Bold

abcdefghijkl
mnopqrstuvwxyz

·

ABCDEFGH
IJKLMNOPQRSTU
VWXY&Z

ABCDEFGH
IJKLMNOPQRSTU
VWXY&Z

·

abcdefghijklmnop
qrstuvwxyz

Melior and Melior Italic

abcdefghij
klmnopqrstuvwxyz

·

ABCDEFGHI
JKLMNOPQRSTU
VWXY&Z

ABCDEFGHI
JKLMNOPQRSTU
VWXY&Z

·

abcdefghijklmnopq
rstuvwxyz

Melior Bold and Melior Bold Condensed

abcdefgh
ijklmnopqrstuvwxyz
1234567890

ABCDEFGH
IJKLMNOPQRSTUV
WXYZ&MN

Es gibt kein Vergangenes, das man zurücksehnen

dürfte, es gibt nur ein ewig Neues, das sich aus den

erweiterten Elementen des Vergangenen gestaltet,

und die echte Sehnsucht muß stets produktiv sein,

ein neues Besseres erschaffen. *Goethe*

Optima

abcdefgh
ijklmnopqrstuvwxyz
1234567890

ABCDEFGH
IJKLMNOPQRSTUV
WXYZ

abcdefghijklmnop

qrstuvwxyz & fffiflftæœßchck

1234567890

ABCDEFGHIJKLMNOPQRSTU

VWXYZ ÆŒ

Optima Italic / Optima Bold

A B C D E F G
H I J K L M N O P Q R
S T C U V W X Y Z
AG St Vi Qu

abcdefgghijklmnop
qrstuvwxyyz & ffifllndngßtttz
$1234567890

A B C D E F
G H I J K L M N O P Qu
R S T C U V W
X Y Z Th

Virtuosa I and Virtuosa II

abcdefghijklm
nopqrstuvwxyz & nde
dgqurxfifttzß

A B C D E F G H
I J K L M N
O P Q R S T U V W
X Y & Z

Ä Th I St Qu
a u e

1234567890

Virtuosa Bold

›ABC‹
DEFGHIJKLM
NOPQRSTU
VWXYZ

£12345 $67890

abcdefghijklmnopqrstuvwxyz

ABCDEFGHIJKLMNOPQRSTUVWXYZ&ÆŒ

abcdefghijklmnopqrstuvwxyz 1234567890

ABCDEFGHIJKLMNOPQRSTUVWXYZ&ÆŒ

abcdefghijklmnopqrstuvwxyz

ABCDEFGHIJKLMNOPQRSTUVWXYZ&ÆŒ

Saphir / Linotype Mergenthaler

𝒜 ℬ 𝒥 𝒟 ℰ 𝒵
𝒦 𝒢 𝒥 𝒦 𝒜 ℳ 𝒩 𝒵 𝒪
𝒫 𝒫 ℛ 𝒫 ℒ 𝒞 𝒴 𝒫 𝒳 𝒴 𝒲

αβγδεζηθικλμνξοπρςτνφχψω
1234567890

*

1234567
890

Frederika Greek / Festival Figures

abcdefghijklmno
pqrstuvwxyz 1234567890

ABCDEFGHI
JKLMNOPQRSTUV
WXYZ & ÆŒQ

ABCDEFGHI
JKLMNOPQRSTUV
WXYZ & ÆŒQ

abcdefghijklmnopqrsſtu
vwxyz 1234567890

Janson and Janson Italic (24 pt. and 48 pt.)

→abcdefghijk

lmnopqrstuvwxyz

æchckfffiflftßœ

→ABCDEFGHI

JKLMNOPQRST

UVWXYZ & ÆŒ

›1234567890‹

Kompakt

¶ abcdefghijk

lmnopqrstuvwxyz

ABC

DEFGHIJKLMNO

PQRSTUVWXYZ

Æ&Th

$ 1234567890

Hunt Roman

abcddefgghijklm
nopqqurstuvwxyyz
cnesffthe

ABCDEFGHIJKLM
NOPQRSTUVW&XYZ
$1234567890

%

The quick brown fox
jumps over the lazy dog

Linofilm Venture

A a B B C Ch D D
E E F F F G G H H I J
K L L M M N N O P Qu
R R S Y Sh T Th U V V
W W W W Wh X Y & Z Z

$ ¢ 1 2 3 4 5 6 7 8 9 0

a b c d d d e e e es f f f g g sh i j k k
l l l l m m n n nd ny o o o of p p p
pf qu qu r r r r s s ss ß ß sh st t
tt the u v w wh x x y y y y & z z

©

Hallmark Jeannette Script

© abcdefghijklm

mnopqrstuvwxyz & pqvyz

áçèñôüff frßthn

&

ABCDEFGH

IJKLMNOPQRR

STUVWXYZ

HZ

$12345678¢90

©

Hallmark Firenze

αβγδεζηθικλμνξοπρςτυφχψω
ΑΒΓΔΕΖΗΘΙΚΛΜΝΞΟΠΡΣΤΥΦΧΨΩ

αβγδεζηθικλμνξο
πρςτυφχψ&ω
»«
ΑΒΓΔΕΖΗΘΙΚΛΜΝΞΟΠ
ΡΣΤΥΦΧΨΩ

'Επαρίστερ' ἔμαθες,
ὦ πόνηρε, γράμματα· ἀνέστροφέν
σου τὸν βίον τὰ βιβλία·
Athenaios

Attika Greek / Artemis Greek

АБВГДЕЖЗИЙКЛМНОПРСТ

абвгдежзийклмнопрстуфхцчшщъыьэюяё

УФХЦЧШЩЪЫЬЭЮЯЁ

абвгдежзийклмнопрстуфхцчшщъыьэюяё

АБВГДЕЖЗИЙКЛМНОПРСТ

абвгдежзийклмнопрстуфхцчшщъыьэюяё

УФХЦЧШЩЪЫЬЭЮЯЁ

История ума представляет две главные эпохи:

изобретение букв и типографий; все другие

были их следствием. Н. М. Карамзин (1803)

Linotype Trajanus Cyrillic

* ا ا ب ب ب ت ت ت ت ث ث ث ث ج ج ج ج

ح ح ح ح خ خ خ خ د د د ذ ذ ر ر ز ز س س

س س س ش ش ش ش ص ص ص ص ض ض ض ض

ط ط ط ط ظ ظ ظ ظ ع ع ع ع غ غ غ غ ف ف ف ف

ق ق ق ق ك ك ك ك ل ل ل ل م م م م ن ن ن ن ه ه ه ه

ة ة و و ي ي ي ي ـ ب ر ف ك ل آ ل ا ل ج ل م لى محمد الله

١٢٣٤٥٦٧٨٩٠

Alahram Arabic

التاجر مجده فى كيسه
العالم مجده فى كراريسه

The merchant takes pride in his purse, the scholar in his books.

*

يا ايها الكتاب سر الى سيدنا الاعز
فسلم عليه بهذه الورقة
التى هى اول الكتاب وآخره
يعنى اوله فى المشرق وآخره فى المغرب

[AN GUTENBERG]

Unserm Meister, geh! verpfände / Dich, o Büchlein, traulich-froh;

Hier am Anfang, hier am Ende, / Östlich, westlich, A und Ω. *Goethe*

Alahram Arabic Shadowed

Ornament is the lyric side of printing, imaginative

and spontaneous, a fresh delight to the eye.

Oliver Simon

Primavera Ornaments / Linotype Janson Italic

(137) Page from the new edition of *Manuale Typographicum*.
Quotation by D. B. Updike printed in Michelangelo.

ABCD
EFGHI
JKLM
NOPQ
RSTV
WXYZ

DANIEL B. UPDIKE * PROGMXIII IS CLOSELY

138

Gilgengart (designed 1938–39)	issued 1940
Alkor music type (1939 for Bärenreiter in Kassel)	1940
Novalis (1946)	(cut, but not issued)
Novalis Italic (1946–47)	(cut, but not issued)
Novalis Bold (1946)	(cut, but not issued)
Gilgengart Initials (1949)	(not issued)
Palatino (1948)	issued 1950
Palatino Linotype Italic (1948)	1950
Michelangelo Titling (1949–50)	1950
Festival Figures (1948)	1950
Zodiac Signs (1950)	1950
Gilgengart II (1940, simplified form for book sizes)	1951
Palatino Italic (1949–50)	1951
Palatino Bold (1950)	1951
Sistina Titling (1950)	1951
Primavera Ornaments (1948–50)	1951
Palatino Italic, Swash Characters (1952)	1952
Melior (1948–49)	1952
Melior Italic (1948–49)	1952
Melior Bold (1948–49)	1952
Virtuosa I (1948–49)	1952
Saphir (1950)	1952
Linotype Janson (1951)	1952
Linotype Janson Italic (1951)	1952
Melior Bold Condensed (1949)	1953
Virtuosa II (1950, simplified capitals)	1953
Sistina Poster-type	1953
Ornamental Rules	1953
Attika Greek	1953
Artemis Greek	1953
Phidias Greek	1953

Linotype Aldus (1952–53)	issued 1954	
Linotype Aldus Italic (1952–53)	1954	
Kompakt (1952)	1954	139
Linotype Mergenthaler (1953)	1954	
Linotype Mergenthaler Italic (1953)	1954	
Linotype Mergenthaler Bold (1953)	1954	
Janson, 24 pt. and 48 pt. (1952)	1954	
Janson Italic, 24 pt. and 48 pt. (1952)	1954	
Attika Borders (1952–53)	1954	
Heraklit Greek (1953)	1954	
Frederika Greek (1953)	1954	
Brush Borders (1954)	1955	
Virtuosa Bold (1954)	1956	
Alahram Arabic (1954)	1956	
Alahram Arabic Shadowed (1954)	1956	
Trajanus Cyrillic (1957)	1957	
Trajanus Cyrillic Italic (1957)	1957	
Trajanus Cyrillic Bold (1957)	1957	
Optima (1952–55)	1958	
Optima Italic (1954–55)	1958	
Optima Bold (1954–55)	1958	
Magnus Sans-serif (1956–58)	(not issued)	
Magnus Italic (1956–58)	(not issued)	
Magnus Bold (1956–58)	(not issued)	
Narrow Linotype Aldus (1959–60)	1960	
Narrow Linotype Aldus Italic (1959–60)	1960	
Linofilm Palatino (1962)	1963	
Linofilm Palatino Italic (1962)	1963	
Linofilm Palatino Bold (1962)	1963	
Hunt Roman (1961–63)	1963	
Linofilm Melior (1965–66)	1966	
Linofilm Melior Italic (1965–66)	1966	
Linofilm Melior Bold (1965–66)	1966	

140

Hallmark Jeannette Script* (1966–67)   issued 1967
Optima Medium (1963–66)   1967
Optima Black (1963–66)   1967
Hallmark Firenze* (1967–68)   1968
Linofilm Venture (1960–67)   1969
Linofilm Medici (1969)   (in preparation)
Optima Medium Italic (1963–66)   1969
Hallmark Textura* (1968–69)   1969

CONTENTS   page

Frontispiece drawing by: Gi Neuert-Hoffmann

This is a revised edition of the Typophile Chap Book No. 37 first issued 1960, which was originally based on the idea of the late Paul A. Bennett, New York, and translated by Paul Standard. Designed by the author, set in Linotype Optima, and printed in offset by Ludwig Oehms, at Frankfurt a. M., and bound by the Ladstetter bindery, Hamburg, Germany.